What People are Saying Abo

I'm so grateful that Seth Kopald shares tl
the world and this short, easy-to-read and practical book is one of
several steps he is taking in that direction. In it, he helps us envision
what Self-leadership might look like in the most important areas of
our lives: in our intimate relationships, at work, as we parent, and in
our spiritual lives. Thank you Seth for this lovely contribution to the
movement.

— RICHARD SCHWARTZ, PhD
Creator and Founder of IFS

Seth has written a clear, concise, wonderful book about how to live a
connected life with yourself and others following a Self-led approach.
I highly recommend this book that applies Internal Family Systems
(IFS) to everyday life.

— MICHI ROSE, PhD, MAT, LMSW

Seth Kopald has written a beautiful book called *Self-Led*. Seth takes
us through ways we can be more Self-led in all aspects of our lives.
He does a beautiful job of inspiring and connecting us to become
more Self-led in the world. Well worth the read.

— KAY GARDNER
Lead trainer of IFS

A simple, clear, and heartfelt little book packed with a lot of power!
By way of concrete examples, explanations, and experiences for
different facets of our daily lives, Seth bestows gentle guidance for

understanding and achieving inner and outer harmony (what we call Self-leadership in IFS). If there was required reading for life, this book would be on the syllabus!

—MICHELLE GLASS
Certified IFS Level 3 Practitioner,
Speaker, and Author of
Daily Parts Meditation Practice™:
*A Journey of Embodied Integration
for Clients and Therapists*

"Self-Led" is an accessible introduction to IFS, showing a path to healing that is grounded in practice and experience. The examples in each chapter are personal and yet universally relatable, and the exercises at the end of each chapter are eye-opening and helpful. The wisdom of this work has corollary principles in other practices and disciplines, and thus can support rather than threaten other counseling or spiritual modalities. What I especially like about this book is how Seth Kopald's wisdom gained from years of teaching and learning shines through in what he's sharing with us.

—TRACY BENNETT
Associate Puzzle Editor and Wordle
Editor for *The New York Times*

Self-Led

Published 2023
Seth Kopald
Exploration Services. LLC
Ann Arbor, Michigan, United States

Cover design by Kathryn Kopald
Book Design by Kathryn Kopald

ISBN: 979-8-9892146-0-0

Printed in the United States of America

Self-Led

Living a Connected Life
With Yourself and With Others

An Application of Internal Family Systems

SETH KOPALD, PhD

Foreword by Susan McConnell

I dedicate this book to all of our parts, to the ones who work so hard protecting us and to the fragile ones who are hiding and waiting for us to come. I know in my heart and bones that they all need our love, attention, and understanding.

A Message From the Editor

I am so honored and excited to have been part of this amazing journey. When Seth originally asked me to join his team, I had no idea what Internal Family Systems (IFS) was. In my role, I had the incredible privilege of not only editing and coaching the development of this book but also experiencing a profound personal transformation in the process. It is my honor to introduce you to this work and offer insights into the remarkable journey it will take you on.

As you dive into the pages of this book, please prepare to delve into a beautiful world of self-discovery, healing, and transformation. The journey within these pages will take you beyond the surface and guide you through the intricate landscape of your internal self. It will not only introduce you to the principles and techniques of IFS but also provide you with a mirror through which you can explore your own role as a parent and the dynamics of your relationships, be it with your spouse, children, G-d[1], co-workers or others within your sphere of influence.

What makes this book truly exceptional is its ability to make complex ideas accessible. You'll find clear explanations, empathetic guidance, practical exercises, and real-life stories that illuminate the path to self-awareness and healing. Whether you're entirely new to IFS or have some prior knowledge, this manuscript will be your trusted companion on the journey toward personal growth and transformation.

I am confident that the words within these pages will touch your heart and inspire meaningful change in your life. The wisdom and insights shared here have the power to unlock your inner potential, foster healing, and cultivate more harmonious relationships.

Prior to this project, I had no knowledge of IFS, and it was through my engagement with this manuscript that I was introduced to my own internal parts. When I reached the chapter about being Self-led as a

---

[1]Changed by the author: G-d is spelled this way because in my tradition, if you write out the whole word, it makes the text holy and this book would need to be treated in a holy way.

parent, I was so emotionally moved that I had to pause my editing for several days. This book has forever transformed me as a parent. I now pause to reflect before criticizing or reacting to the way my children do things. I've become more mindful of the way I communicate with them, and I've learned to speak to my own internal parts when I am triggered by something that I watch my children do. This new found approach has allowed me to parent with less anxiety and more confidence, which is a testament to the profound impact of the concepts you will encounter in this book.

As the editor, I am deeply grateful to have been a part of bringing this work to fruition. I believe it will not only be a source of inspiration but also a practical guide to understanding yourself and others on a deeper level. It is my sincere hope that this book will become a cherished companion on your own journey of self-discovery and healing.

With warm regard and deep gratitude,

Terri King Hunt
Managing Editor
Superior Guidance, LLC

My Message to the Editor

There are some people you meet

Who change your life

Who see you

Believe in you

And literally tell you

You're on a timeline.

I am blessed to have been coached and guided by you, Terri King Hunt, author, teacher, editor, and all around good human. Thank you for walking with me on this path and pointing out all the wonderful things to see. I have grown as a person working with you. This book would not exist without you. Thank you, Terri. Love to you and your family.

Acknowledgements

Although writing this book felt like a solitary act to many of my parts, *Self-Led* would not be possible without various people in my life. First and foremost, I want to thank you, Richard Schwartz, for developing IFS. You have been a mentor, teacher, and friend to me. With confidence and curiosity, you have tirelessly persisted and brought IFS to the world. My life has significantly changed because of IFS. I have a sense of calm and confidence that I did not possess before I learned about IFS and my relationships with my family and friends have improved because of it. Without you, I may have never reached this level of peace and this book would not exist.

I also want to thank all of my IFS teachers: the lead trainers, assistant trainers, fellow program assistants, and IFS colleagues who augmented my understanding of IFS and shined a light for me to follow. Each of you have your own way of dancing within the IFS playground and I value all of you. These lead trainers and assistant trainers include: Richard Schwartz, Paul Ginter, Toni Herbine-Blank, Cece Sykes, Kay Gardner, Susan McConnell, Ann Sinko, Mike Elkin, Mariel Pastor, Einat Bronstein, Chris Burris, Tamala Floyd, Cathy Curtis, Marina Hassanali, Mary DuParri, Jory Agate, Kathy Cox, and Kaitlyn Staeker. Thank you all.

In addition, my clients have been some of my greatest teachers. You taught me what is possible with IFS, how to flow with someone else's system, and that IFS really does create healing and life changes for people. You inspire me to be Self-led and you have taught me how to hold clients and their parts with exquisite attunement. I'm sending a big thank you to all of you.

There are also people along the way who pointed me towards places that I may not have found on my own. Shortly after learning about IFS, I found an experienced IFS therapist, Tanis Allen. Tanis, you suggested that I take the IFS training, and I did. My life changed dramatically from that point forward. You also created an IFS retreat where I spent intimate time with many IFS leaders and felt nurtured by the IFS community. Derek Scott, you invited me to help create a video about IFS and parenting with a group of other IFS parent educators. That experience launched my work with Self-led parenting, which led to me creating the IFS Self-led Parenting Facebook group and many other Self-led Parenting teaching engagements. I also want to thank Toufic Hakim, the executive director of the Foundation for Self Leadership, the not-for-profit side of IFS. You included me on a team of people who helped create a video series to help people during the COVID 19 pandemic. My time with you was very meaningful. Additionally, I want to thank Deran Young for including me in the second Level 1 IFS training offered to Black Therapists Rock members and for inviting me to lead a workshop at the second Heirloom Summitt. You have been a teacher and a role model for me to follow. In addition, I want to thank you, Tammy Sollenberger, creator of The One Inside podcast. You interviewed me a number of times and you helped me become known in the larger IFS community.

As I finished writing *Self-Led*, I approached respected IFS leaders, practitioners, and colleagues and asked if they would be readers of *Self-Led*. All of you took the time to read this book and offered suggestions, insights, edits, and testimonials. So I thank Richard Schwartz, Michi Rose, Susan McConnell, Kay Gardner, Mary DuParri, and Michelle Glass. Not only did you offer amazing insights, you gave my parts what they really wanted from you: your approval and your encouragement. I also want to thank other key readers: Tracy Bennett and Dave Nelson. You are both literary geniuses, who read *Self-Led* from a lay perspective. You helped me clarify passages and you offered help with general structural, developmental, and copy editing. Thank you readers, you helped bring *Self-Led* to a new level.

I want to extend a special thank you to Susan McConnell, developer of Somatic IFS, who wrote the foreword of this book. Susan, you encouraged me and supported me even when *Self-Led* was just an idea. You lit up when I told you I wanted to write a book and my parts noticed. Your support helped me drum up the courage to move ahead and start writing. I'm so thankful that you are the one who wrote the foreword; I am honored and humbled that you agreed to do it.

I would also like to thank my editor, Terri King Hunt. You and I met every couple of weeks and you graciously held my procrastinator and scared parts with love and encouragement. You inspired me to keep going and never judged me when I had months of no progress. Your patience and inspiration was a guiding force as I wrote *Self-Led*. Your understanding of the writing process unlocked doors for me and you coached me every step of the way. I also want to thank Sacha Mardou. You offered many creative insights and helped me open up my creativity which allowed my writing to flow.

I also want to thank my wife, Kathryn, and my children, Ahava, Levi, and Clara, for believing in me and for helping me learn how to be Self-led in my life. Our relationships mean everything to me and I can clearly see how our closeness has flourished as a result of IFS. Kathryn, when I was unsure where to go next in my life, you suggested that I try one of my "cockamamie ideas." That moment of support offered me a freedom I have never experienced. I opened my door as an IFS practitioner and you stood by me as my business grew. You were patient during all the extra hours I spent in IFS trainings and other IFS events. You encouraged and supported me throughout the process of writing *Self-Led* and I can't thank you enough for designing this book by sharing your time and graphic design skills. You set the typeface, developed the look and feel, and designed the cover. It's truly a work of art. To my children, you all gave me permission to write the parenting chapter, which means the world to me, because it signifies that I am the parent you needed. Your permission informs my parts that I am qualified to write about Self-led parenting. In addition, you are the reason I worked so hard to become as Self-led as I am. I want to give you everything I never received and more.

I also want to thank my parts. You helped me and allowed me to write this book. You shared your fears and concerns with me and eventually felt confident enough in me to let this book come to be and go out into the world. I thank you, my vulnerable little ones, for letting me hold you and I thank you, my protectors, who trusted me and graciously sat by and allowed my Self Energy to flow as I wrote this book. It was definitely a team effort.

Finally, I want to thank you for reading this book and for going on this journey with me. I hope I can sense you as you read through these pages and I hope you sense me too.

Contents

Foreword.. xvii

Introduction 1

Parts and Self 5

Being with our Parts 15

Self-Led Intimate Relationships...................... 33

Self-led at Work..51

Self-led Parenting 69

Self-led Spirituality...101

Final words 115

References...121

About the Author 123

Foreword

WHEN SETH ASKED ME to write the Foreword for his
book, within seconds of feeling delighted and honored,
I heard from a part who said I would not do a good
enough job. The part said I hadn't known Seth long enough; I
should have more information about his life...I should be someone
more in every way. As Seth calmly listened to this part, I remem-
bered that what I know, what I feel, and who I am is enough in
every way. In other words, my Self-leadership was restored. I got
from Seth what I know you will get as you read this book. You
will feel Seth's compassionate, understanding presence at your
side, guiding you toward a more Self-led life.

I have been a trainer of IFS since the late 1990s, beginning
with a small group in Chicago and eventually branching out to
bring IFS to the world. What has sustained my commitment and
dedication to teaching this transformative model over the years
has been the people. Seth exemplifies the best of them. I first met
Seth at a Midwest IFS gathering. Or rather, I heard about him
from others, as they spoke of him in an almost reverent tone of
voice, "Oh, *Seth* is helping with...you must meet him." I heard in

their voice and read in their body language that there was something uniquely special about this man.

First introduced to Seth as a helper, I then experienced him helping me as I navigated the technological challenges of teaching during the pandemic. My book, *Somatic Internal Family Systems Therapy*, was published in 2020, at the height of our fear of this novel virus. My ability to teach virtually was also novel. Frankly, I was surprised and overwhelmed by the response to my book with requests for being trained in Somatic IFS. I might have surreptitiously slipped into "semi-retirement." Instead, Seth offered to virtually hold my hand as I taught my first Somatic IFS training.

My part that fears I am not enough shows up in all the areas of my life that Seth writes about. It sat perched on my shoulder with every word I wrote in my book. I doubted I would find a publisher. I could not imagine more than thirty people ever reading it. The IFS model has helped me to bring a compassionate presence to this part and not to buy into its beliefs and fears. I just kept writing another word, another paragraph, another chapter, and it turned out that my book was what the world had been waiting for. I believe the world has been waiting for this book from Seth, too. I am so glad he has done it.

As you read this engaging, informative, and practical book, you will feel Seth holding your hand and your heart. Your parts will feel his acceptance, his wisdom, and his warmth as he guides you through the process of considering the most important aspects of your life—your intimate relationships, your work, your parenting, and your spiritual life—the areas where our parts show up predictably and frequently, pointing us toward our deepest hurts. You will hear his Self-led voice as you read it. Your inner system will feel his attunement as he draws from his own experiences and those of his clients and students in each of the realms. Seth will hold your hand, and his words will go straight to your heart as you enter this exploratory space to find your parts who have created protective shields, parts who have been hidden in darkness, frozen in time, in language patterns, in belief systems, waiting to be found and freed. As the trapped, thwarted energy of burdened parts is found, expressed, witnessed, and released, you will remember that who you are, who you truly are, is enough.

As Seth explains, what our parts need is already inside of us. Yet we also need each other to help free up our inherent Self-energy. Seth has been, for me, a healthy male figure for my "not enough" part that did not get enough of these qualities from a brother or a father. As you read this book, you, too, will find that Seth has packaged all of those qualities. There may be moments when you, too, hear a part say, "Oh, *Seth*..." as you experience his humility, his humanness, his honesty, and his heartfelt wishes for us all to find more happiness. You will feel his fatherly reassurance that when you are Self-led, you can enjoy quality relationships with your own parts and with the important people in your lives. Whether you are a parent, a partner, a clinician, or an educator, you will get the needed guidance and direction to bring the transformative power of IFS to others.

Now, more than ever before, all beings on the planet need Self-leadership. Globally, we are experiencing fragmentations, polarizations, and separations at every level of systems. Buoyed by healthy interpersonal relationships, we can connect with our courage, power, and resilience. We recognize that collectively we have within us the seeds for addressing systemic burdens. This book and the energies, practices, and stories within its covers can bring the liberation of Self-leadership to the places in the world that need it.

SUSAN McCONNELL
Senior Lead IFS Trainer and Author of Somatic Internal Family Systems Therapy

Introduction

Contentment.

Peace.

Confidence.

Courage.

Presence.

THESE ARE ALL QUALITIES we strive for. We spend time and money searching for the right ingredients to feel confident, at ease, and calm through books, workshops, videos, spiritual rituals, exercise, and more. All of these are wonderful things, but what if what you seek is already inside of you?

Perhaps you have heard this before. Peace is within; love yourself, and be the peace you seek in the world. Yet somehow, what is right there seems out of reach. Perhaps that doesn't feel true to you, and you feel alone in this world, disconnected, easily agitated, angry, or feel like you can't seem to get the motivation to do things you want to do. People say, "Just let it go!" or "Don't worry about it," or "Just breathe and be calm." Why isn't it that easy?

I found Internal Family Systems (IFS) during one of the roughest times in my life. I was going through a divorce, and I had heightened anxiety about losing my daily connection with my children and fearing what a divorce would do to them. I put them to bed each night and was a consistent, nurturing force in their lives. I imagined them slipping away, and I had a panic attack in my car. I had a hard time breathing, and I felt hopeless and scared. I pulled over and called my therapist. He helped me regulate and later suggested I buy Richard Schwartz's book, *Introduction to the Internal Family Systems Model.* I ordered it right away. I traveled for work and brought the book with me to read on the plane. While reading, I had a life-changing experience, a crucible moment. I realized that, as a whole, I wasn't anxious. Yet, I had a part who was very anxious, and I was more than that part. I understood I could help that part of me, and my whole nervous system relaxed. I felt the thing I needed, Hope.

The Internal Family Systems (IFS) model, developed by Richard Schwartz, is a framework for understanding our inner world. Rooted in the belief of the multiplicity of the mind, IFS assumes we all have an internal family of parts, all trying to help us live our lives in the best way possible. Just like any family, our internal family can hold various perspectives at once. These perspectives can seem both complementary and contradicting. For instance, you may have the urge to go to the theater to see a movie, yet another part of you may not want to leave the house. You may feel hurt by your friend while simultaneously expressing anger toward that person. According to IFS, we all have various sides to ourselves that are referred to as parts. Our parts can be protective, and they can carry pain. And luckily, we also have a wiser, higher Self, who has perspective, compassion, curiosity, and wisdom (Schwartz, R.C. & Sweezy, M., 2020). We may sense this state when we feel energized, carefree, and insightful. We enter a state of flow, feeling harmonious and engaged in something for its own sake (Csikszentmihalyi, 1990).

IFS helps us build relationships with the various parts of ourselves. Some parts carry pain from the past, and others can overprotect as a reaction to such pain. For instance, in my family, my parents didn't spend much time parenting me. I was on my own, navigating the world. I developed parts who became very independent and capable. However, I became so independent that I had a tough time receiving help from others, and I got angry with people who couldn't help me. Deep down, I felt like I didn't matter. You may get a sense of these different parts of me and how I have struggled in various relationships. Before IFS, I would be taken over by them and not even know it was happening. One part would secretly want help, while another pushed people away. Thankfully, IFS taught me that I, my highest Self, can be there for these parts the way they have always needed. I listened to them, acknowledged what they were feeling, and I offered them help. In doing so, my parts learned to trust me, Self, to be the caregiver and the leader in my system. This type of Self-leadership is the gift of IFS.

When our parts take over, like during my panic attack, we feel ruled by worry, fear, sadness, and more. People trained in the IFS model, including therapists, coaches, teachers, and other practitioners, use IFS to guide people to understand and heal their parts. They also use IFS to help people interact with others in a more healthy way. In fact, this book is about creating healthy relationships with our own parts and with the people in our lives—at work, at home, and in our everyday relationships. In doing so, this book contributes to a critical goal of IFS: becoming more Self-led as we interact with others in the world (Schwartz, 2021).

I wrote this book for you because I believe: being Self-led not only helps you, your parts, and those people in your life; it's one way to bring peace and healing to the world.

Parts and Self

LL OF US HAVE PARTS. We have protective parts and more fragile parts. Our fragile parts, called exiles, have been hurt sometime in the past, and they tend to be pushed deep down inside. Perhaps our parents didn't treat us well or were absent, critical, or aloof. Perhaps kids at school were mean to us, or we had other bad experiences later in life. Through these experiences, our parts take on beliefs or burdens such as *I'm not good enough, I'm too much,* or *I'll always be alone,* and these thoughts create a lot of pain. Especially for children, if people are treating them poorly, they think it must be their fault. Children cannot process that their parents are suffering or going through a life crisis. Their concrete thinking leads them to take on negative beliefs about themselves. Humans do not like discomfort, and so our protective parts come on board to push pain away and to ensure that we stay clear of future discomfort. Those protectors exile the sensitive parts of us. The pain is seemingly hidden until it's not, and we then feel flooded with emotions for seemingly insignificant reasons.

Our protector parts are reactive and proactive. The proactive ones we call *managers*; they try to manage our lives to avoid future pain. They control our appearance, our work style, and how we show up in the world. They also worry, overthink, and can make us seem controlling or overly passive to people around us. They think they have to protect us from feeling what those exiles feel. Our managers don't often know there is a Self inside of us who can handle things. They learned when we were young that we were often powerless to make bad things stop.

When our exiles are triggered, the reactive protectors come—the *firefighters*. They soothe us with activities such as drinking, smoking, sex, shopping, watching shows, or scrolling on our phones. They also numb us out and make us feel foggy or scattered. Sometimes firefighters get activated when our managers have worked too hard, and they need to create balance in our systems (Sykes, 2016). Go-go-go at work, and then drink while watching shows at night.

The key thing to remember is that our parts have good intentions. As Richard Schwartz says in his latest book, there are no bad parts (Schwartz, 2021). Protector parts ALWAYS think they are helping. In fact, they may think they are the only ones who can help. I've heard Richard Schwartz compare protectors' roles to the story of the boy in the Netherlands who stuck his finger in the dyke. The boy was attempting to stop a leak and save the town. I imagine people telling him to go home and him resisting, thinking that if he did, the town would flood, just like our exiles would flood us with their pain. So, as we begin this process, step one is to acknowledge and appreciate our protectors' roles before they will trust us to be the leaders of our systems.

Our parts are considered sacred beings living inside of us. We are born with them, and before any hard times or injuries, they are harmonious and free, unburdened. Yet, as we experience life, they take on beliefs and burdens and start protecting in order to navigate this world. Sadly, many of us have to survive in a treacherous, painful world. So, of course, our parts take over. When our parts take over, we become *blended* with them, meaning they take over our consciousness. We see through their eyes, hear through their ears, feel their pain, think what they think, and feel what they feel (Schwartz and Sweezy, 2020). When we unblend, we can be with these parts from our most natural state—**Self**. Some may call it our highest self, our soul, or our best self. Self has no agendas, only a purpose for healing and wholeness, and has all of the qualities we seek. Richard Schwartz has organized these qualities of Self into 8 C's and 5 P's *(See box 1)*. When we feel those qualities and learn to be with our parts, not only can we comfort them, but we can also build relationships with them, so they no longer feel responsible to save or manage us. They begin to follow and work harmoniously with us as their trusted leader, and we become Self-led. As you read this book, you will learn the benefits of being Self-led.

8 C's	5 P's
Curiosity	Presence
Compassion	Patience
Confidence	Perspective
Courage	Persistence
Clarity	Playfulness
Connectedness	
Creativity	
Calmness	

Box 1: Qualities of Self

What is Self?

When we are blended with our parts, we experience the world from their perspective. It is like we are looking through different lenses that color and even distort our vision. When we unblend, we remove those lenses and see the world more clearly. "When we see through the eyes of parts, the world looks very different than when we see through the eyes of the Self" (Schwartz and Sweezy, 2020, p. 45).

Self is inside each of us; it's our natural state. It doesn't have to be developed or nurtured, and it cannot be broken. Self is an inner healer, teacher, friend, parent, counselor, and ultimate support giver. From this place, we support our parts the way they have always needed to be supported, and we are able to be present for other people as well. "Self is not a passive observer" (Schwartz and Sweezy, 2020, p. 43). Our capacity to love our parts and other people is boundless, and we never run out of what we call Self Energy. Self Energy holds a sublime connectedness to us all. Some may call it G-d's energy[2], universal energy, Chi, or sometimes I refer to it as our life force. We all have it, and the energy is the same in all of us. This book has been brought forth to help us tap into that energy and be with our parts, so we can feel at ease with ourselves and have quality relationships with those around us.

The idea of an authentic Self is not new. Many traditions have shared a similar concept, recognizing a higher Self who is connected to something larger than ourselves. We feel this when we are in the flow, in the groove, or when we feel carefree. Perhaps we feel it when we are in nature or on vacation while spending time with a special person, or during prayer or other spiritual rituals. Some may say, "I'm good," feeling easy and light.

---

[2]G-d is spelled this way because in my tradition, if you write out the whole word, it makes the text holy and this book would need to be treated in a holy way.

You may be asking, "So when I'm not feeling that, I'm still me. Isn't that myself?" It feels like it is, but if we are not feeling curious, compassionate, courageous, and without an agenda, most likely, we are blended with a part. Remember, parts take over our awareness and even our physical body.

When we are Self-led, we don't say hurtful things or cause physical harm (unless perhaps in self-defense). We don't worry or have anxiety. We feel connected to something bigger than ourselves. We feel a sense of presence, clarity, and have a keen perspective. Everyone seems to have a unique experience of being in Self, yet we also sense similar qualities, such as feeling spacious and light. We experience these qualities through Self Energy.

I like to compare Self Energy to water. The water in the oceans, the water in the rivers, the water in the puddle, the water in our bodies is all the same—water. While water can hold impurities, the water is still there, and when it has the opportunity to flow, it usually cleanses itself. Since water is water, the water in all of us is the same. It's the same water that was in every human that has ever lived. Self Energy is like that. The Self Energy that we all have is the same. Even the most inspirational leaders who ever lived have the same Self Energy. They may simply have had more access to it.

With some practice, we become Self-led leaders and caregivers in our internal systems. Our parts, who carry fear, worry, anxiety, depression, sadness, self-criticism, and more, can be cared for by us. Some of our parts, usually the fragile and vulnerable exiles, feel unloved and alone. Yet, when our parts feel our love, they get what they always needed, those things they didn't get from parents and caregivers. And when they feel loved, we get to feel what it feels like to be loved. When we are there for them, we feel their contentment inside, and our protectors no longer need to isolate and manage impressions. Once we are present for our parts, we can also be that way for others (Schwartz, 2021), and our relationships tend to thrive.

Parts Beget Parts

As mentioned earlier, this book is about creating healthy relationships with the people in our lives, at work, at home, and in our everyday relationships. When we are Self-led, we have fewer agendas and are less defensive. When we have an agenda seeking personal gain, people sense it and tend to react by pushing us away. When we are defensive, we invite others to be defensive. If someone walks into the room with a protective shield, we have the inclination to raise our protective shield as well. As we walk on the earth with our defenses down, others can also do the same.

According to IFS, any defensive behavior comes from our parts trying to help us stay safe. We want to feel capable, valued, and accepted. Thus, our managers try to ensure those feelings by making us work harder, say important things during meetings or with friends, or caretake others. The rub is, parts beget parts, and often these behaviors elicit undesired results and unintended consequences. We all have part detectors who can sniff out other people's parts. Those parts sense a lack of authenticity and integrity in others. So when we sense someone isn't being real with us, we resist getting close to them. You may recall a time when someone said kind and polite words, but you felt a different kind of energy coming from them. In response, you may have had protectors who decided to keep them at a distance.

In more overt situations, people may lead with parts who come off as complaining, accusing, or blaming. Again, these parts secretly hope the listener will see the light and give them what they want, usually connection and validation. For instance, in past jobs, if one of my bosses shot down one of my ideas in a meeting, I had a part who stayed up all night creating a well-crafted soliloquy of what to say in their office the next day. I knew they would understand my point if I just explained it again. My part would imagine them looking at me, saying, "I'm so sorry;

you are right. I should have listened to your idea." So at times, I would do just that: set up a meeting and say my piece. To my protector parts' chagrin and to my exile's horror, my supervisor shot something back at me, deflecting the blame and criticism, making me feel worse. What comes next? My angry part came forth, as did my part who wanted to quit and find a new job. From a balcony view, I could see that my boss sparked up my parts during the original meeting. I had a part who wanted redemption and created a "heartfelt speech," which came off as shaming to my boss. My boss probably had an exile who felt not good enough, and their protector jumped up and shot something back at me, which hurt my exile all over again, and so entered my fierce protectors to save the day—the result: a parts party where neither of our Selves were in the driver's seat.

So, whether we are parenting, at work, or talking to our friends or our partners, when we lead from a part, we are inadvertently inviting their parts to respond in kind. And when we feel their parts being activated, ours get even more activated. However, when we are Self-led, our parts can inform us of their concerns, and we can then speak for our parts instead of from them (Schwartz, 2008).

Speaking for our Parts

When we get to know our parts and listen to their needs and concerns, we can represent them well by telling people about our parts. In other words, we can speak for them instead of from them. I often say to my clients, "You can be your part's counsel, like a compassionate lawyer representing their client." There is an amazing thing that happens when we speak for our parts. People tend to listen because their protectors are not as activated. The listener senses that we have their interests at heart because we are choosing our words carefully. As a result, people feel more at ease and more likely to cooperate with us. Just like parts beget parts, when we lead from a Self-led place, the listener's parts can relax, and they have more access to Self as well.

For example, you may feel frustrated with someone who is making you late for an event. If you spoke from your frustrated part, you may say, "You always make us late!" or "Come on! Let's go." Most of the time, the listener will fire something back, and tension mounts. Again, parts beget parts. But if we listen to our part and hear their concerns, you could say, "I have a part that is concerned we will be late, and it worries that people will think poorly of us." That would be received so much better.

People naturally use parts language. We may hear people at dinner say, "I'm so full, but part of me wants dessert!" Or, "I really like the guy, but part of me wishes he would let other people talk." When I was working with a national team consulting for Head Start programs, a federally funded program serving children and families in poverty, we would meet in Washington, DC, three to four times per year. I loved sharing my ideas. However, my boss would often give me praise while the others seemed to scowl silently. I sensed they felt like I was getting all the accolades. It left me feeling uneasy. After I read about IFS, I tried an experiment. I would say to the group, "One part of me totally understands where we are going here and sees the value (and I would give examples), and I have another part that wonders what would happen if we did it this way." 99% of the time, the group would accept my ideas as a possibility and begin incorporating them without the negative backlash. Upon further insight, I realized vulnerable parts of me wanted praise and acceptance, and I had another part, a manager, who was the one speaking and trying to make that happen. He "knew" his ideas were great and proclaimed them eloquently. It makes sense that other people's parts would get activated when that part of me was in the lead. To all my parts' surprise and relief, there was a much better result when they let me lead.

Many years ago, I told this story to a friend of mine who was a manager at Microsoft. A few years later, he said, "Your wizard trick worked like a charm!" I didn't know what he meant until he reminded me I told him the Head Start story and explained how to speak for parts. When I inquired further, he said he used this technique to help his team consider new ideas, and they were able to take them in with less defensiveness. To be clear, we don't talk for parts to satisfy our personal agendas; people would sniff that out and react negatively toward us. We are able to talk for parts when we feel open and curious, with intention and purpose, not hiding a personal agenda.

Our goal in IFS is to be in harmony with our parts, not get rid of them. Richard Schwartz shares that Self is like a conductor at a symphony. When our parts are activated, it's like a cacophony of sound, parts playing their instruments simultaneously, out of tune, with no regard for the others, or even in competition with them. When Self steps up and shows its presence, the parts can stop, get in tune, receive the individual attention they need, and then eventually, with lots of practice, play as one, a beautiful blend of individuals, a sublime synergy.

Getting Started

This book was inspired by my purpose: to bring IFS to the world, to people in everyday life, and to help heal the world one person at a time. I hope that this book will help you be more Self-led in your relationships, at work, while parenting, and in your spiritual practices. In general, I hope this book helps you live a Self-led life.

Being Self-led does not mean we never have parts or we get rid of parts. Instead, we are here for them, and they are here for us, so we live in harmony and cooperation. There will always be times when our external world becomes challenging, we become blended with our parts, and we have a—*parts party*. That's when we feel vexed, overwhelmed, and have contradictory thoughts.

However, by working with our parts and supporting them, we can be more present and experience less extreme reactions. I will offer you theories, examples, exercises, and suggestions that will help you get to know your parts who react to various aspects of your life. With practice, you will find more peace, patience, and perspective, and your relationships will get smoother and smoother as you learn to be with and speak for your parts. As Richard Schwartz often says with a sweet grin on his face, "May the Self be with you!"

Being with our Parts

ONE AFTERNOON, I grabbed a snack between clients. I was eating a tangerine; sweetness was bursting into my mouth. When the client arrived, I put half of the tangerine down for about an hour. When I came back after the appointment, I popped a piece into my mouth, longing for the sweetness again, and experienced a hard shell around it. It was as if it started protecting its own sweetness from being ignored and left alone. Our parts may have had to do the same thing when we were young. How often did we create a hard shell around our sweetness? How much did we have to lock away?

As we begin to get to know our parts, it's helpful to understand that the more we can approach our parts with exquisite attunement and presence, the more they will feel supported and cared for. This is why I chose the words "being with" our parts rather than "working with" our parts. I see "being with" as a deep sense of presence rather than rescuing or fixing our parts. Being with our parts helps them feel our unconditional love, a necessary ingredient for healing.

Being with our parts and ultimately helping them heal may initially seem elusive. As we get to know our parts, it is common to wonder if we are making all this up. We may doubt if our inter- actions with parts are real. We actually have skeptical parts who are valuable protectors who keep us safe. They make sure we don't get conned or drawn into unsafe predicaments. From my experience, those skeptical parts start to soften when they see the work we do with our parts and our new way of showing up in the world. However, being with our parts takes practice; it's a skill to be honed.

Being with our parts is like playing a sport, learning an instrument, or learning any new skill; it takes a bit of practice and consistency to feel comfortable and confident. It doesn't take long to find our way, but it can take time for some of us who have very protective systems. When we practice and intentionally connect with our parts, it gets easier and easier and more natural, second nature even. It's important to know that it is possible for everyone to be with their parts, and it's not something for the gifted few. We all have the capacity to "be there" for our parts. It may take time, yet the payoff tends to be a tangible lived experience: more ease and peace in our lives.

As we turn our attention to our parts, we provide support and build relationships with them. Some see their parts, while others feel them, sense them, or hear them. We may see our parts like a movie in our mind, and as we interact with our parts, we enter the scene looking through our own eyes. We may sense them here with us in our bodies or in the room we occupy. Additionally, we can hear their voices. It may seem like a fleeting thought, our own inner voice, or a unique voice of the part. Oftentimes, parts ˋ will help us understand what they are feeling by telling us or by showing us images or memories. Parts have us feel what they feel. We may feel their sadness, worry, or anger. At times, it can be overwhelming when we are fully blended with our parts, and we essentially become the part. However, as we gain the skill of being with our parts, we learn that it's helpful to feel what they feel momentarily. It is an opportunity to understand their pain and fears. We can then feel compassionate towards them and offer our love and support. We become the ultimate parent, coach, mentor, and leader in our systems. We can give these parts, who are often younger versions of ourselves, what they have always needed: to be seen, understood, supported, validated, and accepted.

The feeling of being seen and accepted is healing. We like to be around people who get us, understand us, appreciate us, and love us. Parts need the same thing and they often desperately seek connection from others in the world. Most of our parts are looking outwards, not realizing that Self exists as a source of comfort. The moment our parts come to know we are here, it is often a healing experience. We can feel the shift in our bodies, a settling. We may become calmer or perhaps experience exuberant joy.

It can easily happen that most of the day, we see life through our protector's eyes. We are blended with them, meaning we experience life through their perspective. Our managers are protecting us, keeping us safe, and helping us experience acceptance in the world. We slip into their roles as they blend with us. However, they are essentially acting out of fear. Perhaps they fear we won't be accepted or loved. Our firefighters keep us from feeling pain and steer us to eat, shop, zone out, watch shows, scroll through our phones, and more. Our protectors are here for us, keeping us safe and out of pain. However, when we are fully blended with parts reacting to fear or avoiding pain, we are not as present and alive as we can be. As we begin to take the lead from a Self-led place, our parts can slowly take it in that we are actually here for them and we are strong enough to handle life.

From an IFS perspective, Self cannot be destroyed, and everyone has a Self who can be a loving and protective presence for our parts. Self can handle anything our parts are carrying; nothing is too much. However, our parts have to choose to give enough space for Self to be here for them. There is a common IFS analogy that Self is like the Sun, and our parts are like clouds. When we are blended, our parts block the Self just like clouds block the sun. Just as the sun is still there, so is Self. Holding this truth offers hope and confidence that healing and living a Self-led life is possible. When our parts are so activated that it feels like a dreary overcast day, perhaps they can just for a moment feel the sun on their backs, sensing the warmth and strength of our love. As time goes by, and we form a relationship with each of our parts, they will let us, Self, shine through.

Unblending

When a part takes over our consciousness, we are blended with a part. We see through the part's eyes, feel what they are feeling, and view the world through their perspective (Schwartz and Sweezy, 2020). This is completely normal and common. We can be taken over by worry, anger, fear, concern, jealousy, skepticism, judgment, and many more states of being. When this happens, we are blended with a part who is feeling those feelings. We are not feeling the C qualities or P qualities of Self listed in the Parts and Self chapter.

I will share four litmus tests for determining if we are in Self or blended with a part. The first two methods are common IFS practices, and I have stumbled on the final two through my own work. First, you can ask yourself if you are feeling the 8 C's; in particular, curiosity or compassion seem to be most helpful. When we feel compassion and curiosity, we have more Self Energy, and when we don't, we often are blended with a part. The second test is to ask: Do I have an agenda? Parts always do; there is a self-serving aspect to their motivation. You might think, "I want this to go my way, the "right" way," or you have an urgency to make something happen. The third method came out of my work with parenting. We can notice how our children and people, in general, are reacting to us. IFS states that parts beget parts, so if people react to us in a negative way, blended with their parts, we can assume we are also leading from a part as well. Mike Elkin, lead IFS trainer, confirmed this for me when he explained something similar with therapists using this model. He explains that if a client has a negative reaction to something a therapist has said, the therapist should pause and see if they are blended with a part before they continue. And if they were blended when they spoke, they should make a repair with their client. Lastly, you can notice where your attention is, in your head or in your heart. Typically, when we are feeling a lot of Self Energy, our hearts feel open. When we are "in our heads," we are usually blended with a part.

1. Am I curious or feel compassion?
2. Do I have an agenda?
3. How are people reacting to me?
4. Am I operating from my head or my heart?

Box 2: Litmus Tests for Self

It's important to build our skill of unblending. We need to notice when we are blended, and we can use the litmus tests above to help us do so. If you are blended, you can ask your part or parts to give you just enough space so you can be here too. You can ask your parts to step aside, hang out on the couch, or even stand right next to you. You can ask them if they want to relax by the beach or in a forest. The key is to follow the part's desires and support where they want to go.

When you feel blended, perhaps annoyed with others around you, ask your parts if they can give you some space and then listen to them. You can let your parts know that if they can unblend from you, you can be with them and offer them support. After you get to know your parts and hear why they are activated, you can return to being with others and perhaps share with them what you learned from your parts, or even just be in a Self-led presence and notice how others react to you now.

Getting to Know Our Parts

Luckily, Richard Schwartz gave us a wonderful tool called the You-turn. When we feel stress, anger, sadness, frustration, the urgency to go-go-go, and anything else that doesn't feel centered, grounded, connected, curious, or all those wonderful qualities of Self—we can do a You-turn. We pause, take a breath, and sense our bodies. We can look inside and try to notice what part is here. We get curious about the reason this part needs to be here at that very moment, and perhaps what it needs from us. This is a skill that may take time and practice, but with persistence, it will become more natural.

In order to get to know your parts, it helps to take a moment and drop more into your heart, sensing parts from your heart rather than your mind. More and more, it seems evident that your heart and gut can interact with you and give you information. When you drop into your heart in preparation for getting to know a part, you will feel more compassion and curiosity.

When we pause, breathe, and notice what is happening in our bodies, we can find our parts (some people don't feel parts in their bodies; that's ok). If someone upsets you, do a You-turn: stop, breathe, and ask, "Where do I feel this feeling in my body?"—tense shoulders, tight chest, stiff jaw? When you sense those feelings, maybe in one spot or sometimes all over, you can assume a part is showing up.

Once you notice a feeling in, on, or around your body, you can direct your openness and curiosity there. If you meet a part for the first time, you can simply focus your attention on that area of your body and ask, "What do you want me to know?" Then just listen and not try not to think. This often results in a message popping into your mind. We may see a memory, hear a voice, or even see a part as it shares what is happening. Usually, once communication is open, we gain a connection with the part directly and can keep the conversation going.

The wonderful thing about noticing we have an activated part is that we gain some separation at that moment, which often offers more Self Energy. By noticing, we are unblending, getting differentiation between Self and the part. This allows for more Self to be present. Richard Schwartz will often say, "Who is the one noticing?" and with a smile, he says, "Self."

When you notice a part, it is important to check how you feel toward it because it's best to get to know parts from Self. Sometimes we are blended with another part as we try to communicate with our parts. However, parts usually won't open up to other parts, because parts have agendas like: *let's get rid of this one,* or *if this part can just stop, life would be better.* That doesn't feel good to our parts, so they stay silent.

If you feel any negativity, like wanting to push it away, apathy, or if you are in your head trying to figure it out, you are probably blended with another part. It's really common to notice a part from a different part's perspective. We have a family of parts inside, and they often interact with each other, and have opposing views with each other. If you experience this, try connecting with the part blending with you and ask if it is willing to let you talk and be with the part you were trying to connect with originally. You might ask it to give you a little space and step back. I like to ask: "Can you give me just enough space so I can be with this part?" Richard Schwartz will often see if a part can go wait in another room. See what works best.

If a part does step back and you don't feel open and curious, simply realize a third part is here and repeat the same process. At times, people can experience part after part after part. That's normal and common. If it gets confusing, it may be helpful to map out these parts and visualize them by taking notes, drawing, or using bubble maps.

When you finally feel open, loving, heartfelt curiosity toward your part, then you can move ahead. You can ask the part about what it wants you to know and simply wait as if you are at a movie, not knowing what will come next. You may see memories, hear them talking, or feel what they feel. Those are all great ways for parts to help you understand them. You can share back to the part what you heard and understood. Share *how you understand,* as well. You know better than anyone else what this part is referring to. You might say, "I remember that too; it was so hard when he was mean to us. We didn't have his support." When you reflect back, you may notice the part responding to being heard, often relaxing.

Also, keep reminding your thinking parts to let you take the lead; they will often start making connections and telling part of the story. Thinking parts try to help create healing or gain understanding, but they often don't allow the part we are trying to hear from tell its unique story. Although you may remember what the part is showing you, or you may understand what it is feeling, it probably holds more than you know. It has its own story and a host of feelings. Our job is to listen, to be there like we always needed. I often ask analytical or cognitive parts if they are willing to help by sitting near me and taking notes, so we can debrief later. 99% of the time, they are ok with that. We are often trained to think through our problems. In this case, you are asking your thinking parts to relax and let you listen to other parts. Then, your thinking parts will actually have more data to process afterward and make more connections.

Sometimes when we are trying to get to know one part, another part shows up and won't step back. If that's the case, we have to shift to that second part and get to know it. This is often true with our main protectors. Perhaps as we try to sit with a tender part, a protector part comes in and pushes us forward and says, "don't look back," or another one comes in who makes us feel numb to any pain. These parts often act as gatekeepers of our internal world, and we need to gain their trust first. By listening, reflecting back, appreciating their roles, and being patient, they will learn to trust us to be with other parts. Remember, these main protectors may not want us to be with other parts who carry pain or who cause trouble in our lives. They often think those parts will take over. Once our protectors trust us and see our power and abilities, they often will let us proceed.

Once we are there with our parts feeling open and curious, and as we use good listening and attunement skills, they will trust us more and more. We are befriending our parts when we pay attention and attune to them. When I think of attunement, I think of tuning in, like a radio. We adjust ourselves to hear and feel what the other is going through. This leads to compassion, feeling for our parts, holding space for them, and understanding how they feel without trying to change, rescue, or fix anything. Eventually, we do help them heal and even retrieve them from bad situations in the past, but first, we need to attune and befriend our parts. Once we are in a trusting relationship, more healing can happen.

Appreciating and Befriending Parts

One way to build trust is to authentically have an appreciation for the work of your parts, especially your protectors. No matter how extreme your parts are, I have not met one that hasn't responded favorably to being appreciated. It's like they think no one gets it, and they are working all alone trying to save your whole system, often with inner critics breathing down their necks. When someone finally appreciates their work, it is as if they let out a breath and say, "It's about time someone recognizes what I'm doing." You can share back how you get it and how you understand that the part needed to do those things (we hold this as a truth for the part, even if we see there are other options for behavior). Once parts feel appreciated and understood, there is room for finding new ways to operate.

As we befriend and get to know our parts, we quite often find our protectors need updating. Since they think it's their job to save us, they don't know the qualities of Self, and they don't often know your full life experience and maturity. Protector parts often started their job when we were too young to protect ourselves. We couldn't use our bodies as we can now. We couldn't choose who to be in a relationship with. We couldn't stop bad things from happening back then; we couldn't move out of the house or leave a particular school. So if a protector started to make us invisible in school so we didn't get ridiculed, the protector might think we are still school-aged children and continue to make us invisible.

After you listen to protectors and you show appreciation for their work, you can ask, "How old do you think I am?" Oftentimes, the answer is younger than our current age. If the part thinks you are younger, say 5 years old, of course, it makes sense they think you can't handle the situation at hand. The answer is not always young, like 5 or 10 years old, which happens a lot; it can be 20's, 30's, or 40's when you are actually older than that. If that is the case, you can ask the part about what was happening back then. It may show you a challenging childhood experience or a time in your adult life, like during a divorce. You can be curious how it was helping you during that time in your life. A part may think it needs to be hypervigilant to keep you safe, thinking you are still young in a bad situation. The part needs updating and doesn't realize how much you have grown since then. You can let it know all about you, your life, and what you are capable of now.

Perhaps you have a protector that shuts you down or numbs you when people get mad. At the time, when you were little, that may have been necessary as being still may have kept you safe or helped you not feel the pain of being shamed by your caregivers. And perhaps, you still shut down or go numb when people are mad. Often, the shutdown part would be thrilled to know you are an adult now and you are stronger, have skills to deal with mad people, and most importantly, you can be the one to protect that little one who needed protecting at the time. Once the protector is updated and sees the courage, confidence, and compassion of Self, it will often be willing to let you go to the fragile, exiled part, the one who is still hurting, still being yelled at, at a particular moment in the past. Once the protector sees you there, caring for that little one, it can choose to find a new way to be of service, especially after you help that part leave and release the burdens they carry. Oftentimes, protectors do their job because they think they have to, not because it's their preferred role.

There are many techniques and complex ways of working with your parts, and being led by a trained IFS therapist or practitioner is a great way to gain such experience. This is especially true if you have complex trauma and have had horrible things happen to you. In those cases, it's important to have a trained facilitator who knows how to help. If you jump to the traumatic experiences in your life without the help of a professional, you can have backlash when protectors get even more protective because you bypassed them and opened up old wounds. However, there are simple things you can do to help your parts, and in-turn feel more alive, connected, and present in your life. First, remember your protectors are trying to keep you safe and have good intentions, and your exiles are scared, lonely, hurting, feeling alone, and need your love and care. In time, when parts get to know you, they will take over less, calm down, and you will feel a sense of ease.

Ultimately, I notice that working with any part is healing to our systems. It creates a ripple effect. For example, when you befriend a protector, and it sees your capabilities, it will move back and allow more of you to be present. Thus, you will feel more alive, lighter, and even perform better with relationships and other tasks. Also, as you help one part, other parts are watching and gaining trust in you as well. So please don't rush. As Richard Schwartz always says, "Slow is fast."

Being with Specific Types of Parts

Many people label their parts based on their behavior. They may call a part their critic, their numbing part, or their angry part. That may be helpful to people for a variety of reasons, and many seasoned IFS people name parts that way. I try not to. Richard Schwartz explains that all parts have a full range of human emotions and are often stuck in their roles. They would rather do something else. A critic may want to be more of a coach. A numbing part may just want to rest and be taken care of. I feel when we label parts by their behavior, we are locking them into that role, and perhaps, we don't take the time to help them release those roles. Thus, I try to say, "the one who criticizes" or "the one who feels the need to criticize," leaving an open door for that part to change when it's ready. Below, I will give some tips for working with or understanding some of the common parts people experience. There are certainly more than I list here. Most importantly, there is no standard way to help a particular part. We need to be open to our parts, listen to them, and ask them what they need from us.

Parts who criticize and self-blame:

Almost always, parts who criticize and blame have experienced criticism and blame from someone on the outside—a parent, teacher, coach, sibling, and more. When we get to know these parts, we often find they are trying to stop us from doing any behavior that will lead to further criticism and blame. So these parts badger us internally to make us better, to make us perfect, so we won't get hurt again. It's really important to honor these parts because they often get pushed away by other parts in our systems. Other parts may hate the ones who criticize and self-blame, or they are afraid of them, isolating the criticizing and blaming parts. That makes them dig in deeper because no one seems to understand what they are doing.

It's really important to find some appreciation for their work in protecting you and share how you understand what they are doing; they are saving you. You can show understanding and help them see you are strong enough to handle things. You can befriend these parts and work together to set boundaries for people who criticize you, and you can help your younger parts who were hurt by the criticism. Ultimately, when your exiles are healed and removed from bad situations in the past, your protectors can relax and take on new roles.

Parts who make us feel numb or spacy:

These parts can be challenging to be with because they often seem elusive. How do I get to know a numbing feeling? Or a sense of spaciness? These parts are elusive as part of their strategy. If they are found out, they may be unable to keep us from feeling pain. They often appear as a cloud, a fog, a wall, or a blankness. First, get curious about these parts. It helps to promise them a few things: you will not try to force them to stop what they are doing; it's their choice when to let you see things, and they can come back anytime. When they understand this, they will often open up to you. You can ask the part if it can share why it needs to keep you blank or foggy. They will often let you know.

My numbing part showed up for me as a cloak. When bad things happen, it wraps itself around me, and I go numb, a flat line response, nothing high and nothing low. As I got to know this part, found out its fears, and built a relationship with it, I asked if it would be willing to lay across my lap and see if I could handle feeling things. I helped this part see that although it was helping me not feel pain, I was also not experiencing joy; I was missing out on life. My cloak didn't really want that, so we worked together, and it learned it can trust me to feel things. To this day, if I am getting close to a painful experience, it shows up, yet it quickly allows me to hang it on a hook on the wall and lets me proceed to experience what I need to experience.

Parts who are angry:
People often have a hard time being around anger, and when a part gets angry, we tend to want it to stop, swallow it, or push it away. We may have parts who don't like the angry one and try to shame it or push it back. People around us don't like it either. We often learn it's not ok to be angry. However, the parts who are angry often have a reason. They have witnessed injustice, unfairness, and criticism; they have been mistreated, and as a result, they have clarity. Parts get angry when they realize we haven't reached our full potential. They are angry because of their mistreatment by people who were supposed to love us and take care of us. Thus, I call these parts: *Truth Seers*. It is important to validate their anger and share how much it makes sense that they are angry. They see the truth, and they are protecting the more fragile parts of us.

It's also ok to let your parts act out their anger inside. I let my angry part flip tables in a room in my mind. We can let them yell and throw fits. They are venting their pent-up energy. You can also let the angry part use your body to express anger without hurting others, our things, or our bodies. You can witness it that way, too. You are essentially saying to the angry part, "It's ok; let out your anger; I'm ok with it. It makes sense that you are angry." Parts will feel seen and accepted. They will also feel that, FINALLY, someone gets it. That's you. What a great way to build trust with these parts. When they feel understood, they often relax on their own terms.

Parts who are defensive:

You may notice when people give you feedback or if they get upset by something you do, your first instinct may be to explain it away or quickly point out what they did too. Parts who do that don't want us to feel the burdens we carry—burdens like *I'm not good enough, I'm bad,* or *I'm too much.* Defensiveness is like a shield, deflecting perceived criticism. These parts may want the attention off of you as quickly as possible, and they want to be sure no one sees you in a bad light. You may have parts who will never let others see you being wrong.

After we get to know these parts and acknowledge why it makes sense that they are protecting us this way, we eventually have to ask them to give us a chance and to trust us to listen to what others are saying. You can show these parts that you can be a learner, you can grow, and it's helpful when others give you feedback. You can also hold the hands of your younger parts who still hold burdens and show your protectors that you can help those young ones feel safe.

Parts who abandon others and walk away:

Many of us have parts who pull us away from people when they hurt us. What a wonderful strategy; we literally move away from the source of pain. We can acknowledge these parts and let them know that we see them trying to help us. They think that if we stay, we will be crushed, hurt too badly, or that our rageful parts might get activated. And we know there are unintended consequences when we pull our love away from people.

It's important to appreciate these parts and pose a question, "What if I could stay and help protect my fragile parts with my presence? What if you didn't have to pull me away?" Again, you ask these parts to trust you to listen to others and respond in a compassionate, even firm way, if needed. You can show your parts that you are strong enough to stay in situations, and you can hold boundaries from a loving place.

Cognitive/Thinking parts:

It is very common when trying to work with your parts to have a part or parts who want to think through your problems or situations. A part may even think about how to approach another part. A part may try to remember the story when other parts show us a memory. It's really important to remember that most of the time, parts won't reveal their story to another part. Doing so doesn't feel as safe because parts always have agendas, albeit positive ones.

As mentioned earlier, if you need to be with a part and your thinking parts are taking over, you can ask the thinking part if it is willing to stand back a bit, giving you just enough room for you to be here, and see if it's willing to take notes regarding what the parts say or show you. Then, afterward, the thinking parts can help you process what you've learned. Thinking parts can gather data in order to make more connections, and they can debrief with us afterward. We need our cognitive parts to make sense of what we learn, but they need to let Self gather the data first. They seem to really like that.

Young fragile parts:

Our young fragile parts tend to be our exiles or young protectors that have been stuck in roles for a long time. When we find young fragile parts, it's really important to first ask the permission of our protectors to see if they are ok letting us care for them. We do this because the protectors have been the ones in charge for a long time, keeping us from this pain. Bypassing them may lead to back-lash, where the protectors flare up and almost punish us for going there. We may get drunk, buy something expensive, fall into a depressed state, etc. If the protectors give us a chance, then we can move toward the fragile ones. If not, we stay with the protectors until we have their trust. If that's the case, you can still tell the fragile one that you know they are there, and you won't forget. You can tell them that you will come for them when your system is able. It's as if someone was lost and then realized people were look-ing for them and knew where they were. The parts gain some hope.

If your protectors allow you to try to help the fragile ones, you can approach them like you would a wounded child or even a wounded animal, slowly, with soft movements, an open heart, and emitting safety from your core being. Sometimes, you can just sit with the fragile parts and let them get used to you being so close. You can allow them to lead, and you should resist jumping to the rescue (that's often another part). When you enter the heartful state of Self, you will intuitively know what to do. Know that this fragile part has been here for a very long time, and if you take your time, it will be ok. Let this little one share stories and memories, and let you feel what they are feeling. Then reflect back to them what you understand and have felt. Ask them to share more until they have shared it all. Then, you can ask the part if they would like to go somewhere else, to be with you or in a safe fantasy place, as Richard Schwartz so lovingly offers.

Again, if you feel overwhelmed by these parts, it's beneficial to seek out a certified IFS therapist for some guidance and assis-tance. They know how to help guide you so you learn the skill of being with, witnessing, and healing these parts.

Consistency

Our parts are not just protecting us from being hurt; they need to be cared for. If we understand many of our parts are younger than us, then it seems logical they would have the typical needs for each developmental age. A five-year-old needs different things than a teenager does. Just as Cece Sykes, a lead IFS trainer, has said, it is normal and healthy to have needs when we are young. Especially in cultures like the US, having individual needs may be shunned. The rugged individualist attitude has unintended consequences on our parts. We exile away our little ones who have typical needs, the need to be held, comforted, protected, and seen.

After we get to know a part, it's really important to keep visiting them and building a relationship with them. The relationship fosters trust that we are the leaders in the system. And these parts can be reinjured if we abandon them. Even if we check in on parts for five minutes a day, they feel some consistency and will often let us take the lead for longer and longer periods of time.

Final note:

Now that we have an understanding of our parts and how to be with them, it's time to explore how to do that in various aspects of our lives. Many people only work with their parts in therapy or silent meditation, which is wonderful. My hope is to help you be with your parts while you interact with the world. Each chapter uncovers how to be with your parts during specific contexts of your life. You will explore how to notice your parts and be with your parts while in intimate relationships, at work, while parenting, and during our spiritual practices.

Self-Led Intimate Relationships

I HAVE TO ADMIT this was one of the hardest chapters to write. My parts thought I must never be in conflict with my partner in order to write this chapter. So I had to come to terms with the fact that I am on a journey: with myself, my parts, and my partner. My parts get activated when there is a risk of being hurt, rejected, and especially—unseen. When the ones I love are upset with me, my parts really get stirred up. Once I acknowledge this truth, I take a deep breath and say to my parts, "I get it. You want me to write with integrity and only teach what I have practiced." I help my parts see how much progress I have made in being Self-led in relationships, and they give me a slight nod of approval to continue writing. So in honor of my parts, I say to you: I am also on this journey, and I don't always get it right.

For the purpose of this chapter, intimate relationships are defined as relationships where our hearts are activated in response to a life partner or potential life partner. Intimate relationships are hard, and they feel like one of the final IFS frontiers for many people. They are landscapes ripe with potential for activating our parts. Remember, when we feel pain, our parts come to the rescue, and it's so easy to get hurt by our intimate partners.

This chapter is not about how to be perfect in intimate relationships and never have conflict. It's about how we get to know our parts, talk for our parts, witness our partner's parts, and do healthy repairs when necessary. Speaking for parts helps intimate relationships have more stability and helps create a safe space for everyone to be themselves. Although the focus of this chapter is not on friendships and casual dating relationships, the same theories and techniques apply.

When we enter relationships, we put ourselves at risk of being hurt, of opening our hearts to someone, and our parts are very leery of reexperiencing any pain they have experienced in the past. Our protectors are on guard, wielding signs saying, "NEVER AGAIN!" Never again will we let people hurt us, and if they do, we will fly into action, fighting, disengaging, or disappearing. Relationships are two circles colliding, two life stories, two internal systems bumping into each other. So the fact that they are challenging makes sense.

Luckily, we learn in IFS that if we take the time to listen and get to know each other's story and get to know each other's parts, we can have compassion for each other, exist in a more Self-to-Self relationship, and support all of our parts. Quite often, when one person's parts get activated, the partner's parts get activated too. Both people are taken over by their parts, often fully blended for hours, days, and even over the course of a long relationship. When I got divorced, I remember having no sense of Self while interacting with my ex-wife; my protectors held firm and often still do. We mainly have parts relating to parts. Luckily, in my current marriage, we both take time to get to know our own parts and share with each other what is happening when we are activated, except for the times we don't—and we both can feel the imbalance, tension, and pain within and among us.

Prior to getting started, it's important to pay homage to the seminal thinkers and authors on this topic. Richard Schwartz, the founder of IFS, shared his ideas about relationships in the book, *You are the One You've Been Waiting For*, and Toni Herbine-Blank designed the Intimacy From the Inside Out (IFIO) trainings along with the companion book with the same title, which applies IFS for use by couples. Both of these IFS experts have influenced my thinking greatly on this topic. In addition, Susan McConnell, who developed Somatic IFS, helped me understand how we are wired for connection with others and how to listen to our bodies when we are in relationships.

Getting to Know our Parts

When we are in intimate relationships, it is completely normal to have parts who get stirred up. In those moments, our parts are often looking outward toward others and pointing their fingers at them. So it helps to remember the Jamaican proverb, "When you point to another, notice how many fingers are pointing back to yourself." There must be parts activated in me if I am pointing at you. So we take a You-turn and see. You notice your body, where you are holding tension, pain, or unease. You pause there and get curious about what is happening inside. If you feel a sensation in your chest, you can ask your chest what it wants you to know. The part residing there will often come forward and share. Ask your parts: what else they want you to know, how they are trying to help you, what are their fears if they can't help you this way, and how long they have been doing this job? If you sense a fragile part, you can be with it, hold it, and let it tell its story.

You see, our parts are situated in the past, and they are experiencing prior hurts and painful situations simultaneously with what's happening at the moment. As our partners yell at us or criticize us, it may activate an exiled part still being yelled at or criticized by a caregiver in the past. Our protectors may arise, just like they eventually had to do in response to those times. They may shut us down, make us scream, make us please the other, or run away. As Toni Herbine-Blank says, "we are trying to get the past out of the present" with this work so we can be with what's happening right here and now. From that place, we gain more curiosity, compassion, and less pain.

Intimate relationships typically stir up our most fragile exiles because most of our wounds come from relationship wounding, such as not feeling seen, loved enough, or understood. We may have been emotionally or physically hurt by the very people who were supposed to love us unconditionally. As humans, we are hardwired for connection, and we need relationships and belong-ingness. When we don't get it growing up, we start to believe we are not good enough, we are too much, or we are not worthy of connection. Our exiles take on these burdens and blame them-selves. Then a team of protectors emerge to keep us away from those vulnerable feelings.

Some protectors act as people pleasers or caregivers to try to win people's love, or we develop parts who tell us we don't need anyone or can't rely on them. We may have protectors that become very defensive to criticism because criticism shines a spotlight on how worthless we feel. We also develop firefighters who may make us feel numb, distracted, or rageful. We also may have parts that make us stomp away, or ones who turn to drugs, alcohol, infidelity, and countless other ways our protectors take action.

When we step back and gain perspective, we are able to track how our parts become activated when our partners hurt us. There is usually a cluster of parts who come to the rescue, one after another, often in rapid succession. It helps to notice our initial, automatic reaction. When our partner says something hurtful, what is the immediate feeling? Do you feel hurt or sad? And then what: anger or the need to flee or shut down? What comes next: irritation, frustration, or the need to explain, correct, or teach? As you observe these parts, try to open your heart and sit with them, listen to them, and even let them show you memories that are meaningful. We start to learn our parts' stories, and most importantly, we can be there for them the way no one has before, the way they have always needed. In those moments, let your parts know how you understand by sharing examples and how you remember those times. Notice how parts soften as they feel seen and understood. Let them know how you want to be there for them moving forward. When you finally get it and know their stories, then you can tell your partner all about your parts and the way they are feeling. In IFS, we call those courageous conversations (Herbine-Blank and Sweezy, 2015).

Talking for our Parts with Courageous Conversations

Unless you are jumping straight to this chapter, talking for your parts is not new to you. When we talk for our parts, we first listen to them, feel what they are feeling with a compassionate, open heart, and invite them to show us what they want us to know. Then we speak for them as a representative and their advocate. We might say, "I have a part who felt really hurt when you yelled. It thinks you don't love me when that happens, and one of my protectors wants to get in the car and drive away, while another part wants to yell back." We may notice there are no accusations here, no blaming or shaming, just information for the other person. When we share this way, the listener can feel compassion for us and our parts and, hopefully, feel safe enough to look inside themself and see what their parts want us to know. Talking like this often softens both people and encourages more closeness and intimacy.

When we talk for our parts, we are more Self-led, which feels safer for the listener. Remember, if we blend with a part and speak directly from it, the listener's parts are called forth to defend and protect, and they fire right back. So either person can take the first step of looking within, witnessing their parts, taking a breath, and speaking for them. It's not easy, however, to be the first one to unblend because our parts are so ready to protect us from feeling hurt. It takes courage to be the one to pause, be with your parts, and speak for them. It is an act of true courage. We have the power to hurt or cause harm, but we also have the power to create peace and connection; in that space, we have access to our highest wisdom.

Toni Herbine-Blank refers to two people speaking for their parts as being in a *courageous conversation*. It's courageous because, in a sense, we are asking our protectors to trust us, to trust Self to take over, to be vulnerable in the midst of a storm, and to take a risk in lowering our defenses. I like to remember what Richard Schwartz often says: Self cannot be harmed, and if we can ask our parts, who feel fear, to hang back, we can be courageous in these situations. When we are Self-led, we can sense this truth: the bigger the reaction from our partner, the bigger the pain underneath. When we are compassionate to their pain, their reactions simply make sense and don't feel so hurtful. Even the most extreme behaviors are rooted in a person's pain. However, that is not an excuse to cause injury to another person. It's extremely important to find physical and emotional safety if you are in danger and if you are in a physically or emotionally abusive relationship. As Richard Schwartz says, "All parts are welcome, but they are not welcome to cause harm."

When intimate partners are not getting along, either person can request a courageous conversation. They may not use those terms, but one person must initiate. That often entails pausing, checking inside, and unblending from your parts enough to feel the desire for reconciliation. You might say, "Is now a good time to talk?" Or, "Is it ok if I share what's happening for me?" It's often important to ask permission when you want to share what's happening for your parts. When the other person says, "Yes," there is an opening, a willingness to listen. When we don't have permission, we may activate the other person's protectors. It's important for the listener to be ready to listen, and it must be ok for your partner to share that now is not a good time. The key is for the other person to hear our parts' stories and to understand our parts' needs, so they must be ready to listen.

Examples of Courageous Conversations

I'd like to share an example of a courageous conversation that happened between a couple that came to me for couples' communication coaching. This cisgendered, straight couple had a conflict when the woman had a conversation with another man, and the husband had a reaction feeling she was flirting. They both started the session visibly upset with each other, bickering back and forth. As both of them took turns getting to know their parts and unblending, it became clear that both of their arguing protectors were between 11-13 years old, with their own stories to tell. They shared with each other what their parts were experiencing, and as both realized their preteen parts were the ones fighting together, they softened and even chuckled at the reality of all that. Both unblended and gained perspective. It was such an illustrative example of how powerful this model can be for people.

In a different session with the same couple, the woman shared the story about her part who shuts down when her husband gets angry. She shared how this part began its job when her father was angry, and how this part shuts down to avoid feeling hurt. The husband then shared how his part gets angry when she shuts down, feeling like she is deserting him. They both exhibited curiosity and compassion for each other and agreed to speak for their parts in the future. She agreed to say, "I'm starting to feel like my part is shutting me down. Can we pause?" And he agreed to pause when he is angry and be with his part, to help his part settle down, and then talk for his part so her part doesn't have to shut down. He also agreed to speak for his other parts, who get hurt and angry when she starts shutting down. They both seemed energized by realizing this familiar communication pattern might change; they felt hope.

I'd also like to share another example that illustrates how illuminating it can be when two people share their parts' stories. My wife and I sometimes fall into a familiar pattern. I try to be "helpful" by offering suggestions, and it rubs her the wrong way. A lot of people have fix-it parts who activate other people's protectors. I would get angry at her defensive reaction, not understanding the response to my "loving offer." One day we had a courageous conversation. She went inside and found a part who showed her times throughout her life when she was criticized for her behavior. She then noticed a more fragile part who was made to feel not good enough. She shared that when I step in to help, it activates the one who thinks they're not doing it right and, therefore, not good enough, and her defensive part comes to the rescue. I felt softer toward her defensive part, and my heart opened to her fragile one. I could feel the Self Energy growing in my body. Then I went inside, and a part showed me the time when I was 13 years old, and I decided to clean the garage. When my mom came home, I was so excited to show her. Her only comment was wondering why I didn't clean the high shelf filled with heavy camping equipment. It felt like a punch in the stomach. I realized I developed a protector from that instance. This protector looks for things I miss when I do things and lets me know, so I can fix them, keeping me from criticism and pain. Then it was clear to me that the same protector does that for people I care about. It sees what they are doing wrong and tries to help. The problem is, when people experience this part of me, they don't feel helped; they feel criticized as if I am taking away their self-efficacy, and I don't trust their abilities. As for my wife, this action sparks her into action. By having that courageous conversation, I had a big aha, and although I'm still trying to help that part trust me to take the lead, I've reduced the frequency of extending my unwanted "help." My part wants to help so I will be loved. However, I usually get the opposite reaction from people when that part takes over.

So how do we know if we are Self-led enough to have courageous conversations? We can check to see if we have the C qualities of Self; we can notice if we have an agenda, and we can determine if we feel an urgency to say something. If so, pause and be with your parts. Once you feel more grounded and with more Self Energy, you will feel less defensive and more curious about your parts and your partners' parts. This will be a signal that you are ready to have such conversations.

It is also important to sense whether or not your partner is Self-led enough for such a conversation. If one person shares intimate and vulnerable information and the listener is not able to respond with open-heartedness or curiosity, the speaker's parts can be very hurt and may shut down further communication in the future. Below is a helpful guide to having courageous conversations.

HELPFUL GUIDE

Steps for Courageous Conversations

1. Notice if you are blended with parts.
2. Unblend if necessary and get to know your parts. Listen to their stories and help them feel understood and seen

---

by sharing how you understand what they are showing and telling you. Check to see if you are getting it right.

3. Think about how you want to speak for these parts and what information you want to share.

4. Assess how much Self-Energy you have and whether or not you have to unblend from more parts to have a Self-led conversation.

5. Extend an invitation to the other person, asking if they would like to have a conversation. Many people would like to know what the conversation will be about ahead of time, so they can prepare themselves by being with their parts. You can ask the person if they are willing to have a conversation about a specific topic (e.g., the fight we had at dinner) and ask if it's ok to take time to listen to their parts before you both start talking.

6. Determine if they have enough Self-Energy to receive you. Look at body posture and sense if they feel open to listening.

7. Speak for your parts and tell their stories without blaming and shaming the listener. You can say, "When you _____, I had a part who felt _____ and reacted by _____." For instance, you can say, "When you spoke sharply, I had a part that felt hurt and reacted by shutting down." You might add, "Then another part got angry." You can also share how old the part is, and even where it is at that time (e.g., Standing in the living room, being yelled at by Dad).

8. The listener then shares what they understand, and the speaker can give clarification where needed.

9. The one who was listening can also share what happened for their parts during the same situation. We

> may need to give our partners time to get to know their own parts first.
>
> 10. While listening, notice how your body is reacting and encourage your parts to let you (Self) stay and listen. If you become blended, you may have to say to your parts, "I can handle this; if you trust me to be here and listen, it will be ok. Please give me just enough space so I can stay here."
>
> 11. Again, as the listener, it helps to share back what you understand, just like you would to a part, and see if you got it right.
>
> 12. It's important to remember that these conversations are challenging, and we are not always received by others the way our parts wish. It's most important to assess the safety regarding sharing our young parts' stories. If the listener reacts negatively, there can be more hurt feelings. So take it slow.

When having courageous conversations, it may help to remind your parts that there is a difference between intent and impact. When your partner shares how they have been impacted by your behavior, we may be quick to say, "I didn't mean to hurt you" or "That's not what I meant!" But it's best to remember there was an impact, even if you didn't intend one. Your partner's parts were affected, and it's helpful if you can hold space for those parts and understand their feelings. You can certainly say, "I see what I said really hurt you." When attempting a repair, please don't say, "I didn't mean to yell, *but* you yelled at me," the word *but* often negates what was said before, and telling them what they did takes away from your repair. You can help your parts see: impact is not a reflection of your worth but an indicator of how your partner's parts are hurting based on past, painful life experiences.

In some cases, when tension is high and your parts won't unblend, it can feel impossible to have a courageous conversation. If that's the case, I highly recommend seeing an IFS therapist or practitioner who is also formally trained in IFIO. They can beautifully walk you both through the process, where you both first get to know your own parts. Only then can you have a courageous conversation and speak for them.

Doing a Self-Led Repair

We all know relationships are hard. Since our parts are often near the surface, we will inevitably become blended and say and do hurtful things. Although that is certainly human, when we don't make a repair, those wounds we create sit and fester, and our partners' pain is not metabolized. One of the greatest gifts you can give to your partner is making a heartfelt repair. Making an apology tells your partner's parts, who are worried if they are lovable, that indeed they are and that they are not the cause of your hurtful behavior.

When you sense that you hurt your partner in some way, you can acknowledge you were blended, you spoke and acted from your parts, and caused harm. You can apologize for saying hurtful things, and you can share how you are aware your parts took over. We acknowledge the impact our parts had on their parts. We may say, "When my frustrated part took me over, I said hurtful things to you. I can see I activated your parts and caused you pain. I'm sorry. Would you like to tell me about how you and your parts were feeling?" As you listen, hold your own parts' hands because they may get activated too.

When someone initiates a repair, it's important to be with your parts, who may want to blend and lash back. Your parts may have been holding hurt and anger. You can help your parts see the other is doing a repair, being vulnerable, and that means they love you. Then you can say, "I'd like to share what my parts were feeling when that happened. Are you ready to listen?"

Often, as we experience someone offering a repair and we feel more spacious, we realize we also had parts who played a part in the conflict. If so, you can do a repair as well. As mentioned earlier, one way to know if you are Self-led or blended with a part is to notice the reaction of others to your behavior. Before your partner said or did those things, perhaps you were distracted or led by a well-intentioned manager who was trying to "get things done" when your partner responded with frustration. Perhaps you activated your partner's exile with your lack of attunement. If so, it's helpful to acknowledge that as well.

To be clear, we must be responsible for our own parts in the end. If our partners trigger us, we must be the ones to notice what's happening inside and understand our parts. We cannot blame other people's parts for our hurtful behaviors when we are blended. We can notice how the other person's parts affect ours, but ultimately, it's our job, or even a manager's job, to make sure we do no harm.

Getting Our Needs Met

When we don't take time with our parts, we often don't get our needs met. We may stay in caregiver mode or in isolation. And when we don't get our needs met, we often lash out or pull away further. It is completely normal and healthy to have needs. Having courageous conversations helps us get our needs met. Yet we often push our needs aside, feel it's selfish to have needs, or we bury them, feeling hopeless that our needs will never be met. When our needs are not met, there is a festering of parts that goes on. Some may feel resentful, hurt, unseen, angry, or that there is no place for me. So we hide our needs, and our protectors take over, often with anger.

It's important to note that anger is not inherently a bad thing, and we often recruit a team of our managers to help us suppress our anger, or our firefighters suppress the anger in self-harming ways. We can honor our anger and listen to our angry parts. Our angry parts are often teenage or younger parts who have recently awakened to the realities of their own family and how they have been treated. Typically, they are angry because of how they have been treated. These parts are truth seers. They know what needs have not been met. We can let these parts know how it makes sense that they are angry.

Anger is justified from the part's perspective. That doesn't mean we need to blend with the anger and act out from the anger. When you tell your angry parts how you get it and why it makes sense that they are angry, they often find some ease and feel more understood. Conversely, when we are Self-led listeners, we can hold space for our partner's anger, especially when they speak for it, instead of from it.

Personally, my exiles and protectors get activated quickly when someone displays anger toward me. After being with my parts, I have learned that others' anger feels like a lack of love, and because love was so tenuous in my house growing up, my parts are very threatened by anger. Anger means no love, and my needs won't be met. In fact, my parts often misread people's facial expressions and interpret discomfort as anger, and get activated if I am not right there with them, reminding them. "It looks like they are angry, but they may be hurting or upset about something else." My parts can go from 0 to 60 really quickly when someone displays anger toward me, so I often have to pause, breathe and take time away to settle down and gain perspective with my parts. When I finally do, I talk for the parts and share how they were activated, and make a repair if needed. When this happens with my partner and me, she often reciprocates in kind, and closeness can resume.

When we are living through our protectors' eyes, they embody us, and we become the anger, the hurt, and the disappointment. When we do this, our partners' protectors will get activated as well, and the cycle deepens. Our protectors often judge our partners, so their protectors take over too. It becomes a parts party fast if we are not careful. And, Self begets Self. So if you can ask your parts to give you just enough space to be here and let you be in the lead, you will notice your partner's parts will relax, too, and you may be surprised by the loving interaction that follows.

Finally, being with and loving up your own parts teaches you how to be with your partner in a loving way. If you can treat your partner and their parts with the exquisite love and presence you give your own parts, their parts will soften back and allow their Self to emerge. And when that happens, all of your parts can be held in loving energy from both of your systems. This reminds me of a time I provided an IFS Zoom workshop to a spiritual community in the Himalayas of India. As we started, I realized they had only one computer for the whole group, and I wanted to see everyone's faces. So I said, "As you look at the screen, if you can see yourself, I can see you too." I saw a man lean over to another person and say, "Did you hear what he said? If we see our Selves, he can see us too?" That is the essence of IFS regarding relationships: If you can be with your parts and they allow your Self to come forward, others will be able to see you, your essence, and respond in kind.

Self-Led Communication Ritual

I designed this Self-led Communication ritual, and I offer it to you as a framework for having a loving, parts-sharing experience with your partner. The intention of this ritual is for you and your partner to understand each other more deeply and have an opportunity to resolve any conflicts or tension in a healthy and loving way. Come to the ritual with an idea of what you want to talk about and preferably come up with an idea of what parts you want to speak for or speak about.

HELPFUL GUIDE

Self-Led Communication Ritual

1. Find or create a calming, safe space. Perhaps light candles or play soothing music. Create an atmosphere that feels good to both of you.
2. Start by "going inside." Breathe deeply and notice how your body feels. Notice what parts are present, whether you are blended or more Self-led. Here are some ideas for identifying parts:
3. Think of a topic you would like to discuss and see what part of your body reacts (e.g., tension, pain, uneasiness, etc). Breathe into that area of your body and see if you can notice a part there.
4. Sit quietly and notice what messages you receive and be open to seeing which part is trying to get your attention.
5. Ask yourself, "Do I have an agenda for this ritual?" If yes, see which part has that agenda. Example: If I sense an agenda to make my partner stop doing something, I will get to know why my part feels that way, and then ask that part to let me be here and be with my partner.
6. Find a part of you who needs you to speak for it. Have the intention that you want your partner to understand this part and why it reacts to things the way it does.
7. Take turns and help your partner know this part of you (or a cluster of parts who work together). Share what you

---

know about this part, how it perceives the world, things it says, how it makes you act when you are blended with it, and things that activate this part.

8. As the listener, you can share back what you are hearing to see if you understand this part.

9. Share any compassion you may have.

10. If your partner's part seems like a protector, you can ask: How does this part help you? What is it afraid will happen if it doesn't help? What does this part want me to do?

11. If it is a fragile part (exile): Reflect back on how you sense what their part feels. Ask how old it is. Share any warm feelings you have for this part. Ask if there are things that you do that hurt this part. What else does it want you to know?

12. Show appreciation and gratitude for learning about your partner's part/s and do any repairs that come from your heart.

13. Go back inside yourself and thank your own parts for showing up and sharing. Spend time letting them know what you learned about them and things you may do to support them.

14. Make sure both of you have a turn to share and listen.

15. Find a way to close the ritual: you might decide to hug, read a poem, or make an intention, for example.

Self-led at Work

WHEN YOU HEAR the word "work," what happens in your body? Do you feel tension or hesitation? Do you have a part that wants to run? Do you have a part that wants to jump in and get to it? The word "work" seems to conjure many different feelings for people. *Work* may feel synonymous with have-to's and shoulds, and often leads to the *dowannas*. I dowanna work. We may also have parts who believe we need to devote ourselves to work, so we have success. Those parts have often experienced scarcity of some kind, like if you or other family members grew up with less money and resources than you needed.

And if I ask: What do you want to do for work? You will probably say: I want to be challenged, inspired, and stimulated. I want work that encourages me to bring my best Self forward. When we find that place, work doesn't feel like "work," and we often experience a state of flow. We become pleasantly lost in our work, like when we are doing a hobby that we love.

So what's the problem? Why are so many people unhappy at work? Let's face it, being in the workplace is one of the most challenging places to be Self-led. My doctoral studies in organization management and leadership inform me that it is very difficult for people to be themselves at work and to feel Self Energy. At work, we have people over us who can make decisions about our lives and tell us what we can and can't do. Work environments may feel physically and/or emotionally unsafe. We may be working with people who activate our parts. Many of us feel the need to perform so that we can feel worthy in other people's eyes. I bet you can sense these parts I'm alluding to, the protectors who work hard, and the exiles who will feel those vulnerable feelings if we fail.

There is a benefit to creating climates of psychological safety where people feel accepted, respected, valued, and heard. When businesses create such a safe space, people become more comfortable, and their protectors can relax. When their protectors relax, people at work tend to have more creativity, innovation and are freer to speak up with ideas and concerns. In such a climate, leaders have more access to a diversity of ideas and clear data to make informed decisions that lead to thriving businesses.

Even though external factors such as toxic work conditions and threatening hierarchy are common, when we build relationships with our parts, we gain the power of choice. We can choose how we respond, and even how we internalize what we experience at work. When we are blended with our parts, we are essentially taken for a ride, and even if our parts have good intentions, there are often unintended consequences for their choices. We may overwork and damage our relationships at home, or we may get sick from pushing too hard. We may get overly defensive in a meeting and say things we regret. There are many examples that we could add to this list, moments when a part took us over, and we needed to do something and later realized—ugh, I wish I had a rewind button.

It is important to note that being Self-led does not mean we find ways to be ok with mistreatments such as microaggressions, overt racism, sexism, and other assaults on our identity. When we are Self-led, we can hold clear boundaries and speak up in an effective way when we are harmed. We take action, and we step into the fire of truth.

Being Self-led at Work

My passion for engagement, intrinsic motivation, and love of work has been a continued force for me and has steered my topics of study. Until my senior year in high school, I couldn't find my way in school. I had no motivation for formal learning and had little direction in life. I struggled to get a B (3.0) average until the day my English teacher, Mr. Diedzic, wrote this on the board: *Knowledge is Power.* I sat up in my seat; something stirred in me.

I see more clearly now how powerless I felt in my life at that point, and my parts yearned for something greater. Mr. Diedzic began by using fantasy and science fiction novels to prove knowledge is power. All of the main characters who maintained their autonomy, sense of Self, and empowerment followed this doctrine. They sought out knowledge, had information, and with it, were able to be in control of their own lives. A switch turned on, and I got straight A's effortlessly from that point forward. I was thirsty for an understanding of any kind. The part of me that resisted school stepped back, and I became curious and confident as my newfound studious craving intensified. Being in Self allows us to walk into our power and opens our curiosity and creativity. And with knowledge and understanding, we gain perspective, one of the qualities of Self.

As I studied education at Michigan State University, I learned what it means to be fully engaged in learning, and this increased as I became a Montessori teacher. Dr. Maria Montessori shared that when we are in a state of concentration, we reach our highest potential as a human, integrating our minds and hands into work. Mihaly Csikszentmihalyi (1990) describes this phenomenon as the state of flow. So naturally, as I turned my study to organizations and leadership, I wanted to know what it means to be fully engaged at work and sensed that we as humans would be much better for it if we were.

Being Self-led at work helps people fully engage. When we have more Self Energy, we are curious, confident, courageous, creative, and we have perspective, persistence, and presence. When our parts sense these qualities, the ones who hold self-doubt and insecurities seem to take a step back, and our protectors who try to help us by procrastinating, being overly defensive, or by shutting down are also not so charged. When those parts trust us and let us take the lead more frequently, we naturally show up, share our ideas, create new and innovative solutions to problems, and connect with people collaboratively. We don't feel threatened. As we build relationships with these parts, we gain choice; we can ask these parts to let us take the lead rather than remain blended.

Although it seems like we can't change the external world, when we get to know our parts, noticing when they are reacting and taking over, we can find some sense of Self, and suddenly, the world around us changes. Those who seemed adversarial are now seen as fellow humans walking around with their own messy system of parts, just like us. During times when I was Self-led, I have seen people who I thought had unbendable extreme beliefs soften and consider new ideas. I also realize people aren't judging me as much as I thought. Consequently, I am more free to be myself at work. When we are present and Self-led, we achieve what our parts want: we perform well, we have good ideas, we get along with people, and we find our passions at work.

How to Be with Our Parts at Work:

We will always have parts at work, but being with parts is very different from being blended with them. When we are in meetings or talking to our boss, our parts may easily become activated. The skill we are developing here is one of awareness and compassionate response. You may feel a stirring in your belly, a tightness creeping up your neck, pulling on the base of your skull, or other bodily sensations. All these physical signs steer us to our parts. If you don't resonate somatically, you may notice your impulses: the desire to run, the urge to fight back or become invisible, or even the pressure to acquiesce by relinquishing your power to the hierarchy. Pause there and breathe. Do a You-turn and see who is here. Ask your tense neck what it wants you to know, or put your hand on your belly and let that scared or anxious one know you are aware of it. This is the beginning of coming home, of Self embodiment (McConnell, 2020). Imagine if you had a wise, loving sage inside of you, comforting your parts. That sage is you, and you certainly have that capacity.

When these parts come forward at work, notice them and then ask them to tell you what's happening, to tell you their story, and remain as curiously open-hearted as you can. If you find yourself thinking about or making connections for this part, you may need to ask your rational and thinking parts to relax back and let the parts tell their own story. Even though a part is showing you something from your past, listen to your parts as if you don't know the story, because you don't. Your parts have their own experiences and take-aways that you may not remember. Being seen, witnessed, and validated is healing, and your parts need that from you. Listen with a beginner's mind.

Parts may tell you or show you memories about times in the past when they were hurt by others, and the present-day situation may be stirring all that up. For instance, I recently noticed I have a part that does a lot of self-promoting in front of people who hold power over my standing. As I got to know this part, I realized it wants a few things. It wants to ensure my place in the organization so I can maintain my connections, and it thinks if I get the approval of the one in charge, it will guarantee my standing. As I listened more to my parts and sat with them, it hit me; I wanted the leader's approval, like the approval I secretly wanted from my own father. Upon that realization, my system softened, and I could be with the part who needs approval. I give the part what it always wanted: attention and reassurance that I won't abandon it. My self-promoting protector also relaxed, noticing that when I am here with the younger part of me who needs approval, it doesn't have to seek it from the outside. So I sit in the meeting, sensing the younger part, letting it know it's ok. Consequently, I can stay in my seat and contribute meaningfully to the conversation at hand without inserting self-promoting comments that derail the innovation that could have come forth. In the end, working with our parts is a service to the organization within which we work, and we get self-healing in the process. Not a bad return on investment, eh!?! All the stakeholders benefit.

Conflicts with Others at Work

Work environments can be fraught with external factors that challenge us. Conflicts with others at work are certainly common and can surely activate our parts. People may talk over us, do things behind our backs, disagree with us in front of others, or overtly confront us with a range of intensity. Some people may act like they are better than us. Others are consistently late, miss deadlines, and lack thoroughness. Parts of us may view some people at work as toxic. In general, all of these behaviors that activate our parts come from other people's parts, and our parts are reacting. Parts tend to elicit parts in others, no matter the context.

Why do people's parts get so activated at work? One thing we do know: many of our reactions are our protectors doing their jobs with good intentions, as they fear the worst will happen if they don't. What will happen? That's a good question to ask our parts.

EXERCISE

Get to know a part regarding a conflict at work

1. Take a moment and imagine a person at work who activates your parts. In your mind, let them do that thing they do, and notice what happens in your body. Take some time with this feeling and really sense it. Keep your attention there and ask that area of your body, "What do you want me to know, see or feel?" Perhaps you hear a voice say, "I hate them!" Or, "I wish they didn't work here." Perhaps, a part says, "I'm scared of that person." The part may also have you feel things like rage, nausea, or fear, or it may show you a scene where the person looks like a horrible villain.

2. See how you feel towards that part of you. Do you feel open-hearted towards it and curious to learn more? If not, and if you feel the need to explain it away, convince the part to be positive, or if you have any negative feelings toward that part, notice that another part of you is blending with you in this moment. If so, you are feeling what they feel and are seeing what they see. Perhaps another well-intentioned part is helping you be positive. If that's the case, ask this blended part to give you just enough space so you can be here, or even invite it to go relax, if it wants to, in another room. Now see if you feel

---

more open-hearted toward the part of you who we started with and see if you are curious to know its story. If not, repeat the process until you do. The key to getting relief and clarity is letting the parts of you tell their story without feeling judged or criticized by other parts inside. They need to feel accepted and understood by you.

3. Once you're there, ask the original part, "Can you tell me or show me why you feel this way when the person at work does what they do?" Once the part shares what it wants you to know, take a moment and share back how it makes sense to you so it feels seen and understood, and ask it to show you more, again and again, until you have the whole story.

4. Ask the part if it likes you being here, listening, supporting, and attending to it, and notice its reactions. This is the beginning of a relationship.

5. Ask the part, "How are you trying to help me?" It may tell you it avoids that person, argues with them, or outshines them. See if you can appreciate what this part is trying to do and why. Then reflect that back.

6. Ask, "What would happen if you didn't help me this way?" You may hear about something catastrophic, like: "We would be destroyed," "We would get fired," "We would feel shame," or something else. These answers tell us about the fragile material underneath, about our exiles who feel we aren't good enough, we are too much, or we don't matter.

7. Then we may pause and be with that feeling, with that vulnerable part and let it know you are here for it too. Deeper healing can happen with that part if you work with an IFS therapist or practitioner, and you can even

learn to do it on your own after a number of sessions with a skilled facilitator. In the meantime, let the part know you will be back to tend to it when you are able.

8. Once you learn the part's story and understand why it was reacting, thank the part for sharing and commit to spending more time with it. You can also start speaking for it.

Coworkers tend to listen to our feedback when we can speak for our parts, instead of from them. You may say, "A part of me was frustrated when you cut me off during the meeting. While I can see you were excited by your idea, my frustrated part felt like I got interrupted, and I wasn't able to finish sharing my thoughts. Then another part of me shut me down. Next time, can you please let me finish before you jump in?" This type of sharing usually elicits understanding in others and produces less shame and less extreme responses in others.

In addition, when we build more relationships with our parts, we often avoid many conflicts at work because we are not starting them. It's common that our parts with the best of intentions take the lead and say things we think people will become excited about, yet leave them feeling put off or irritated. Remember, our parts are serving us. They may appear helpful and prosocial, but there is always an agenda to keep us feeling confident and safe. So when they take the lead, usually there is some unintended consequence. Personally, as a talkative person, I realize that when I'm more Self-led, I talk less in meetings and wait until there is something really important to say for the good of the group, not to advance my own standing.

Leading Groups or Teams

As a team leader or a manager of people, being Self-led is invaluable. When we aren't, conflicts arise, and the work suffers. As a leader, I certainly have experienced times when my parts were so activated that I turned others off, and they turned against me. I let my defensive parts run the show, and I was so blended that I felt like Self had left the building. The more my parts dug in, the worse things got. Since then, I have learned how important it is to pause and be with my parts when I feel threatened or criticized. When we are blended with our parts while in a place of power, like a team leader or a manager, things can get ugly pretty quickly.

As a leader, we must lead by example. We model how to be with our parts and ask them to let us (Self) take the lead. On the outside, people will see us pausing during conflict, considering our words, and leading with clarity and with compassion. Currently, positive organizational psychology teaches us the importance of being our best Self while leading, and so does our personal experience—we get results. When we are Self-led, people have the space to be more engaged, share more ideas, and cooperate more readily.

When people feel threatened in any way, they need to defend themselves. Sometimes they have primal responses to fight, flee, freeze, or fawn. When this happens, we have less access to our creativity, innovation, clarity, and even our comprehension. So, as leaders, we need to create safety so people can perform their best. When we are Self-led, we become curious about people's ideas, set a tone for welcoming everyone's voices, and we encourage the best in people to come forward. We notice when people have personal needs and attend to them. We look for openings to hear from everyone. And we start to see our own biases and shortcomings and learn new ways of being in the world with our fellow humans on our teams. In the end, the organization benefits from teams led this way.

One key skill I've mentioned again and again is the power of pause. When we lead teams, there are many moments when we are hit by emergencies, pressures from above, or from our stakeholders. In those moments, our parts will often take over and try to "fix" the problem because they have fear. Fear that we will look bad, or worse, we will be fired, banished, or even ruined. Again, our tender parts underneath hold those concerns of not being good enough or feelings of unworthiness, and our protectors are valiantly trying to keep us away from impending doom. Then, as we pause and notice who is here, we can be with these parts, hear and validate their feelings, and let them know we can handle this if they give us some space. When they do, we gain access to our inner wisdom and clarity. Personally, I have learned I can be confident in most situations if my reactive parts can step back. I start to see solutions to whatever problems I face. We simply have more access to our brain power and our intuition and insight when our parts cooperate and let us lead. Even in situations that can't be fixed or solved, we react much better when we are Self-led.

Client: Jared

One of my clients, who I will refer to as Jared, works at a small tech company and leads a team of people. We've worked together for over two years. Recently, Jared reported that his company was not making their numbers. There was a fear running through the organization that they may have to shut down if things didn't improve. Many people in the organization were spinning with stress. The good news: Jared shared that when he met with his team to debrief, they all seemed positive and hopeful, and they said things like, "We can figure this out; we'll do what we have to do." He commended them for their positive outlook and shared his gratitude. And they let him know, "We are doing what you do. You model this for us." In essence, he is now more Self-led at work, when prior to IFS, he would have shifted into high power, fix-it mode. He would have pushed people, and himself, to solve this problem in a stressful way. Since he has more Self Energy, he is more calm, clear, and confident, which allows his team to be more at ease. Thus, their protectors relax, and his team has more access to their highest level of problem-solving, creativity, and innovation. When we are Self-led, we function better, and we can solve more of the problems our parts are stressing over, so it helps them if they allow us to be in the lead.

•　●　•

Leading up

Leadership doesn't always happen with formal authority. People can lead upward within teams and in organizations. Oftentimes, when we are Self-led, we may be the only ones who can see through the fog of chaos or see the forest through the trees. We may feel calm and have perspective when others don't. That's a great time to lead up, to step forward and share your thoughts, help the team calm down with your presence, and drop some wisdom that may take the team in a new direction. There is a leadership theory called servant leadership (Greenleaf and Spears, 2002), and it was based on observing the influence of Sherpas helping people climb Mt Everest. When the Sherpas were there, things went smoothly, even though they said very little. When they left, the group fell apart. Sometimes, our calm and confident presence can help a group and our leaders stay focused and clear-headed. And I have found when we are Self-led, we can hold up a mirror to our leaders, share feedback, and create change when necessary.

We can lead upward by example: when we are more Self-led, those around us can be too. I have personally experienced my supervisors or team leaders soften and gain more openness as I increase my curiosity, compassion, and confidence. Leaders are people with parts, and they benefit greatly from Self-led people around them. Their parts relax, and we also get to see their best Selves.

Top Level Leadership

Many of us assume effective top-level leaders are superhumans who have all of their stuff together. However, they have parts too, and when we say it's lonely at the top, it's true. Top-level leaders often have many manager parts who help them look confident and sure of themselves, even when they aren't. It's threatening to show vulnerability, fearing that others will lose confidence in them. Therefore, it's extremely common for managers and top leaders to fall into organizational defensiveness, feeling they must always be right, have a handle on things, and hide mistakes (Argyris, 1990). Their manager parts take over, fearing they will not be seen as competent and worthy of their position. Oftentimes, this means they block other people's valuable ideas, and the organization suffers.

When leaders take the time to be with their parts, they gain more qualities of Self. They have more clarity, perspective, compassion, courage, curiosity, and persistence. They become someone others want to follow. Leaders don't exist without followers, people who see the leader's vision and feel confident to step forward with the leader. Leaders inspire others, connect with people, and have integrity—they do what they preach. Conversely, managing tends to be more contractual: you do what I say, and you get paid. Manager behavior makes sure things get done.

Typically, managing and leadership behaviors are seen very differently, although a manager can and should demonstrate leadership capabilities.

Chris Argyris, a former Harvard professor, was a seminal researcher and professor on the subject of what it means to be a leader. He helped the world see how prevalent defensive behavior and thought plague leaders and consequently strip them of their effectiveness. He noticed that time and time again, leaders of organizations protect themselves from being seen as not knowing the answers. They create defensive walls around themselves, quieting peoples' voices, shutting down contradicting opinions, and even creating organizational structures that limit their exposure to being seen as weak. In the end, this backfires. Leaders are then seen as egotistical, power-hungry, closed to ideas, and elitist. And worse, the organization suffers greatly from shutting down peoples' innovative ideas and contributions. The leaders lose the eyes and ears on the ground and limit the diversity of thought when solving problems. Argyris (1990) suggests that leaders essentially ask their defensive parts to step aside and help create a work environment where peoples' voices are welcome and valued.

Many books and articles have been written to try to encourage organizations to lean into a growth mindset and become a learning organization (Senge, 1990). We know that for leaders to appear open to peoples' ideas, they have to try some of the people's ideas some of the time, not all of the ideas all of the time (Detert & Burris, 2007). Trying everyone's ideas all the time would lead to chaos. A good leader has a balcony view perspective and sees how ideas will affect multiple systems within organizations. The key here is that healthy leaders don't feel threatened by not knowing things, and will encourage others to help them see when they miss something. A Self-led leader views people's feedback as a gift for themselves and the organization. And, if you are a leader, you can tell your parts, "We look good when the organization is thriving, so being open to people's ideas helps us too."

One aspect of effective leadership is trusting others to do what they do best. In order to have trust, we must first look inside and listen to the parts who are scared to give up control. We need to understand their fears and what they think will happen if we lose control. We may sense a feeling of overwhelm, even terror. As we sit with those feelings, we may begin to see images or scenes from the past as our parts show us how they learned that not having control is dangerous. Those parts are still in the past, experiencing those troubling times. Hiring a trained IFS therapist or practitioner would help greatly in these instances to help guide you through it.

Another key aspect of leadership is having a vision, the ability to imagine what the organization can be in the future. This clarity lies in Self Energy, and when we are Self-led, we have the capacity for vision (Schwartz, 2021). As our parts begin to trust us, we have access to the full capacity of our brains and to something more—wisdom. In IFS, we believe that when we tap into Self Energy, there is a collective wisdom there. Perhaps it's what William James thought of as our stream of consciousness, his belief that we all share a central consciousness. In IFS, we believe there is a shared wisdom in our collective Self Energy. When leaders have access to this collective wisdom, it's as if they have more than their own facilities at hand. They are given understanding, like a download from somewhere else. Perhaps it's just an openness to possibilities, yet I often experience such gifts when I'm with my clients, assisting in a training, or even while interacting with my family. It often feels mystical.

Another benefit of Self-led leadership is the creation of spaces where shared decision-making is possible. We all know that one person rarely has all the answers, and multiple perspectives are helpful in making decisions. More and more, organizations are unveiling their biases toward diverse people and thoughts. We are in a time of awakening and social change, and if organizations don't adapt like an organism in a shifting pond, they will die.

As leaders take a step back and decenter from the conversation, diversity of thought can fill the room and the minds and hearts of the decision-makers. People younger than us, people from different cultures or genders, know things we don't, and they can help us see what our clients and customers need and want from the organization. When diverse teams share in the decision-making, not just in the data giving, the decisions themselves reflect more of the people receiving your services or products. Thus, in the end, we are not only contributing to creating a just world, but we are also contributing to creating a thriving business that serves its stakeholders.

How to be a Self-led Leader

We all have parts, and we should not see them as bad or as something to get rid of. They are protecting us; we should offer them love and help them feel appreciated for their work, like a good leader would. However, when they blend with us, our vision is distorted. We see things through the eyes of the ones who have been hurt before and are desperately trying to never let that happen again. So, we make proclamations that others scratch their head at, feel punished by, or even oppressed by. Our protectors desperately try to avoid feeling pain, feeling shame, and losing our standing in the world. Yet, when they know YOU are here, the ultimate inner leader, Self, they can relax and learn it is truly safe to follow you. When you are able to lead your own inner team, then you can lead the organization with Self-led leadership.

We can be with our parts who come up when we are leading others. Imagine a time in your life when you wished someone, anyone, your parents, a teacher, or a coach would stop, notice you, sit with you, and ask, "Hey, what's happening with you?" then intently listen, show they understand, and reflect back what they hear validating your feelings instead of giving advice, fixing, or shaming you. Wouldn't that be healing? When we feel heard and understood, we feel supported and can often tap into our own resources or ask for more help. So, we are this way with our parts. Take the time to notice where they show up in, on, or around your body, and listen to them. Be that person you always needed.

Then in meetings, on calls, or during stressful times at work, notice when they are stirring or taking you over, and remind them you are here. Let them know it makes sense they are concerned and that you will take care of the situation at hand. You may notice a sense of peace and openness come over you as the parts step back, unblend, and give you the lead. Then as you interact with others at work, people will sense your openness, compassion, and curiosity. Conversations will be smoother, and you will gain their trust, engagement, and willingness to follow your lead.

As Richard Schwartz says, if parts don't give you space, that's a good "trailhead" for further exploration and relationship-building with your parts. At home or with an IFS-trained professional, you can get to know your parts better, why they need to protect you this way, and which vulnerable parts need protecting. Trailheads are gifts, a beginning of healing, an opportunity for growth. Following them leads to better relationships inside and out. Remember, you have to be a good leader inside before your parts will let you be the leader you want to be on the outside.

Final note

Leaders, be with your parts and see if they will let you take a step back into the circle of humans at your organization. Ask them to let you see people as wise Selves, bountiful data gatherers, and co-leaders helping the organization thrive. Practice this in a meeting and watch the magic happen. See the light bulbs start to go off and see the employee satisfaction levels start to climb as people feel seen, accepted, and heard. When you have a different way of seeing things or even a disagreement, speak for your parts rather than from them. Doing this will help create a climate of openness to people's ideas and suggestions.

Even if you don't officially manage people, know that you are a leader as well. You can model how to be Self-led. By moving through your workspace this way, others will be more open to your ideas and more likely to collaborate with you. By speaking from a Self-led place, you can shift the tone of a meeting when you see people's parts popping off. You won't be so activated when your coworkers are acting out because you will see their parts struggling, and you will have patience and compassion for them. You will offer people a reset button created with your compassion and perspective. As you hold your parts, you can also hold the group.

Self-led Parenting

A S I WROTE THIS CHAPTER, I had parts who worried I would be a fraud, espousing things that I didn't do myself. They could see where I was falling short in my parenting and demanded that I get IFS therapy to make sure I was more of a Self-led parent. So I did. Otherwise, they wouldn't have let me publish this book.

As I commenced on this journey, my daughter and step-daughter were in college, and my son was a teen in high school. My son and I have always been close, yet during his teen years, his protectors seemed activated around me. He shut me down for giving suggestions and often rolled his eyes and walked away. I had parts who sometimes lashed out in response, protecting me from feeling hurt. In addition, I can get overstimulated easily; he tends to like big movements and makes loud sounds. I would often make comments to make him stop. And finally, he had parts who challenged me when I tried to teach him that peace and kindness were the way to go. He even told me that if he were in Star Wars, he would be on the Dark Side! I couldn't accept that, and my parts were struggling to make him "see the light."

As I got to know and helped my own parts, I realized I was often correcting him and telling him to do things differently. So, of course, his protectors had to block me. He wasn't feeling accepted. When I spent time with my parts, I realized it was me. My parts needed him to be a certain way, so I would be ok. I needed peace and calm, and I wanted to be seen as a successful parent. Once I spent time with my parts and really understood what they needed from me, my parts relaxed, and I became curious about his way of being in the world.

When I consistently showed up this way, his parts relaxed too. I found myself more quiet, more interested in what he was doing, and more accepting. To my parts' surprise, he started helping around the house, sought my attention in positive ways, and his compassion and sweetness had room to emerge. One day, my parts couldn't help it and asked, "How could you be on the Dark Side?" He turned to me and, with a soft, wise voice, said, "Dad, there couldn't be the Force without the Dark Side." In that moment, my parts understood. He wasn't really on the Dark Side; he just needed me to understand him. Our relationship deepened further, and we have a lot of tenderness with each other. He models kindness and has the biggest heart of anyone I know.

During the same time, my daughter had become a young woman who needed freedom and space to explore the world. Being in college during the pandemic was counterproductive to those desires. She had to return home, and we both reverted to her high school days. My parts set rules out of fear; her parts were annoyed and wanted to break away. She felt trapped, literally in quarantine. Over time, as I worked with my parts and she moved back to school, our relationship shifted: we became two adults who enjoyed hanging out together. We've always had a natural ease with each other, and now it was free to flourish in a new way. As I showed love by supporting her freedom, she became curious about who I am beyond my dad parts. Our closeness deepened in ways my parts couldn't imagine.

IFS also helped me form a deep and loving relationship with my stepdaughter. She was a tween when we met, and my parts really wanted her to like me. I had to ask my parts not to be overbearing. I noticed when they gave me space; I gave her space. At the same time, I was always right there with an open door for her to walk through. I greeted her when she walked into the room, and I allowed my curiosity to guide me. I was interested in the things she was doing and offered my support when I thought she needed it. I noticed that her protector parts, who were strong when we first met—keeping me at a distance, softened when they got to know me. They settled in and let her Self be in our relationship. We spend hours talking and laughing. I am so lucky to have another daughter, and our relationship is very strong.

Parenting is Hard

As a parent, you likely feel the responsibility to raise your children in a way that seems right and better than the way you were raised. You may feel pressure to create helpful, productive citizens with good manners. You want them to be successful individuals; however that may be defined by your family culture. We all raise our children with the tools we have: the examples left by our parents. We implement the strategies that worked well, avoid those which did not, or we give our kids what we never received. Let's face it, parenting is really hard, and we often feel guilty about how we raise our children. This chapter may bring up those parts in you. If so, I hope they can sit next to you and feel your comfort. Please reassure those parts that you are doing your best and that as you read on, you will learn new things that will help your children grow and thrive.

With no roadmap, we do what we think is best for our children. However, as we look inside ourselves, it's important to determine *who* thinks it's best. Which part? We often blend with parts of us who run the show, and parts always have an agenda with limited perspective (even if they are helpful and have good intentions). If parts are leading while parenting, there are often many unintended consequences.

As stated earlier, there is a Jamaican proverb that states, "When you point a finger at someone, notice where your other fingers are pointing." There are always three fingers pointing back at you. This analogy is helpful for many applications. In the case of parenting, I often say: as we point to our children when they are "misbehaving," not doing enough, or not doing it right, we probably have at least three parts activated in us. Perhaps we have a part who believes the child isn't listening, while another part is angry, both parts protecting a vulnerable part who believes we are a bad parent if our child acts this way. Under close inspection, we often find that the goals we have for our children serve our own systems. We want to feel better or avoid discomfort, so our protectors make demands on them.

Most parenting strategies tend to focus on things we can do to help our children change their behavior or their actions. Perhaps these strategies encourage us to speak in a more support-ive way, thereby helping our child shift their behavior. Yet, feel what that implies. If I tell you I'm helping you change, grow, or do better, what does that bring up? Resistance? Feelings of inadequacy? Anger? When the parenting message is "you must change," the subtext is: I don't accept you the way you are, and you must change to deserve my approval (my love). The child will often feel they are too much or not enough, which are common burdens our exiles carry. Yes, it is important for us to guide our children. However, when parts lead, we often send the wrong message to our children, even when we lead with kind parts. If the message is: I'm helping you improve, it means the child is not good enough presently. And when children feel those feelings of not being good enough, their protector parts rush forward. They become defensive, avoidant, angry, withdrawn, or even inauthentically compliant.

As we travel through this chapter together, we will discover the power of Self-led parenting. With increased perspective and openness, we will gain insight regarding how to be with our children in a way that supports their natural development in all areas.

Parents' Parts Beget Children's Parts

When we talk to our children from a part or when we are blended with a part, they will often feel the need to protect themselves in subtle to extreme ways. If we are blaming, protectors will need to block or defend. If we are manipulating, protectors may need to flee, push back, or ignore. These helpful protectors keep the vulnerable feelings of exiles from bubbling up to the surface. Thus, when we parent from a part, it is as if we are handing our children an invitation to react to us from a part, as well. Without realizing it, we are contributing to the behavior we hope to avoid.

For instance, I have a part that believes there is a right way to do things in the kitchen. That part has honed skills in what it thinks are the most efficient, safe, and effective ways to prepare food. When my kids were teenagers and began cooking in the kitchen, this part got all riled up and corrected their actions by offering "helpful" suggestions. This part took over and showed them how to do it. Another part thought it was my job as a dad to teach them, and I had the right to insert myself. However, can you guess their response? Yes, they rolled their eyes, stiffened up, got short with me, and began to push back harder! Another one of my parts got offended and snapped at them because they were being so disrespectful. Notice it was my helping part that started this chain reaction. They experienced their dad saying, "You're not doing it right!" Perhaps even, "You never do it right."

My daughter would often come home to visit when she was away at college. When she would visit, she would offer to make food for the family. If I went into the kitchen to offer a suggestion, one of her protectors would stop me in my tracks and say, "I got it, Dad!" Since then, I have learned to help that part relax, and I leave the room to give her space when she cooks. I also feel a sinking feeling in my belly as I notice a part in me who imagines my children's parts sharing these types of stories regarding why they feel like they aren't good enough or why they can't trust themselves. And that part feels a bit better when my daughter texts me pictures of the food she prepares. I can tell she is proud of her creations.

When I am Self-led, I'm with my parts, who feel urgency or anxiety when my kids cook. My parts are afraid they will mess up the kitchen or burn the food, and I'll have to fix it. When I have enough space from those parts, I get curious about the way the kids are doing things in the kitchen. I wait and see how it works out. I have even learned a trick or two from them. I give space for them to be, to follow their own lead, and to trust it will be ok. They end up learning what works and what doesn't in a self-directed way, without the added pressure and judgment from my parts.

Being With Our Parts Helps Our Children

As parents, we affect how regulated and Self-led our children can be in our presence. I like to think that parents are like the weather, and the children are like barometers. Barometers measure the atmospheric pressure and the weight of the air. Have you ever noticed the weight in the air when people are upset or fighting? How does your body react to that pressure? Similarly, the parents' systems affect the atmosphere in the house, and with close observation, we can see children reacting to the amount of pressure they experience. The felt sense in the room can be associated with the level of psychological safety children experience. Psychological safety refers to how safe it feels to show up without consequences to self-image or status (Kahn,1990). In other words, how it feels around others determines if we feel safe or not to be ourselves in their presence, whether or not we will fear being judged or shamed. When the climate of the home is threatening or unsafe, children's protectors will be present and ready to do their jobs. If children feel judged, corrected, accused, watched, or at risk in any way, subtly or overtly, they develop burdened exiles and protectors because our behaviors as parents send messages of their worth and lovability. We can also be easy with our parts who parent this way. Most of us were hurt during our upbringing, and we have developed protectors who take over when we parent. Those protectors think they are helping.

On the positive side, when we pause and ask our parts to give us space, we can be present with our children. When we are Self-led, we are relaxed, curious, confident, compassionate, and calm. At these times, children sense openness, room to breathe, support, and connection. In response, their protectors can relax. Those are the moments when we feel a connection with our kids.

Another analogy I have created to demonstrate this is as follows: imagine your child is a little boat on a vast ocean, and you are the ocean. When it becomes stormy, and the ocean's waves rise and fall unpredictably, the little boat is tossed around, unable to control itself. When you feel turbulent, notice what happens to your child. Like the tiny boat, they are tossed and turned, seemingly out of control or without direction. Their behavior usually upsets us more. In those moments, we often yell at our children, demanding that they get control of themselves. It's as if we are saying. "You need to calm down so I can be ok!" Can you imagine how hard that would be if they were the boat in those types of waters? It's almost impossible for them to steady themselves first. When we get space from our parts who are upset, and we feel inner calm, it's like the ocean settles and the boat rights itself, now in calm waters. Then, the boat can go on its normal course. When children seem out of control, take a pause and notice what's happening inside. Calm the ocean and observe what happens.

When we are Self-led and have cared for our own parts, we can attune to our children more readily, just as we do with our own parts (Schwartz, 2021). We see our children clearly without judgment, and to be seen and understood is healing. Our children learn their needs will be met and feel accepted for who they are and for their diversity. When we are curious, we allow children to be different from us and to have unique beliefs and ways of operating in the world. We readily notice when children need assistance rather than perceive actions as misbehavior.

With curiosity, we seek to understand. What is happening with my child? Perhaps they are hungry, nervous, anxious, or scared. Focusing on the need allows us to respond supportively rather than reactively. It is normal and healthy for children to have needs. When we respond negatively to their needs, children take on burdens or feel like they are a burden to us. When we respond positively to their needs, they feel supported and can often learn self-regulation.

Understanding Child Development

The way we respond when children have needs can affect how they view themselves and the world. Erik Erikson's stages of psychosocial development align with IFS nicely. He believed children develop positive views of themselves (psychological well-being) when the adults around them respond supportively. When we are born, we move from total dependence on others to more and more independence. Dr. Maria Montessori, the first woman physician in Italy's history, transformed early childhood education in a way that demonstrates a deep respect for observing and following children's needs. For instance, Dr. Montessori believed the gestation period for infants is really eighteen months rather than nine. Nine months in utero and nine months out. Just like in the womb, newborn infants need consistent nurturing and care because they cannot care for themselves. Usually, around nine months, infants can begin to sit up, become mobile, and can put food in their mouths.

Infants and toddlers

During infancy, our responses affect whether our children feel safe and taken care of. Erikson suggests that in the first year of life, we develop trust or mistrust. If our needs are met, we can trust the world. If not, we learn that we can't. In other words, we begin our lives with normal and healthy needs which should be met without distress. IFS clients often find exiled infants carrying burdens when their basic needs have not been met. Infant parts can hold burdened beliefs, such as they are unloved, unworthy of love, or should not express needs. Anecdotally speaking, my clients and I have found exiled infants crying alone, shaking in severe distress or fear, and stuck in time. When Self goes to these infants, the infants show or tell the story of being left alone or being scolded for having needs. The infants usually settle rather quickly when Self gives the babies what they need at the time—attentiveness and holding.

From a Self-led parenting perspective, when our frustrated parts emerge when babies are fussy, we can ask those parts to give us just enough space so our compassionate, calm, and patient Self can be with them. When we feel calm and compassionate, we see that infants settle as well, just like the boat on a calm ocean. When my daughter was an infant, before I knew of IFS, I would hold her each night to help her fall asleep. I found that if I held her while standing, played soft music, and bounced her with a soft dropping feeling, she would be soothed. I imagine that dropping sensation as feeling momentarily weightless, perhaps as soothing as floating in the womb. My daughter would often fight the sleepiness as my legs burned and sweat dripped down my spine. And, if I let frustration blend with me, she showed immediate signs of discomfort and would be more alert. I noticed this and experimented with pretending I was in a cozy space drifting off to sleep, my body emanating comfort and ease. I would let my eyes slowly close as if I was falling asleep, she, in turn, would relax, and I could feel her sink deeper into my arms and finally drift off to sleep. I would sit in a rocking chair, resting my body, and let her go into a deeper sleep before laying her down. I was her calm ocean.

My son enjoyed similar motions, yet he really felt soothed outdoors. When he started to cry, I would take him outdoors and show him how I understood what he needed. I walked him around the little circle path from the house to the sidewalk and back. He looked up at me as if to say, "Thank you, Dad, for understanding me." When we are Self-led, we pick up on babies' subtle cues, and when babies feel seen and understood, they can be at ease. When their needs are met, they learn that they can trust the world.

According to Erikson, if infants develop trust and continue receiving attuned support, they become toddlers who develop autonomy. Trust allows them to feel safe enough to take risks with confidence. If we allow children to explore without harsh repri-mand or overly cautious blocking, children are less likely to develop feelings of shame, doubt, or guilt. For instance, a toddler may dump a tub of crayons on the floor gleefully. Our parts may get triggered by what seems to be a blatant sign of disrespect. However, the toddler is simply exploring and experimenting. When we react negatively, they learn such natural inquiry is wrong, and often feel they did something to anger the parent. Instead, we can find opportunities for toddlers to dump things, perhaps items that cause less concern for you as a parent. You may fill a container with toys or blocks so they can dump things as much as they want. The message is: I see your natural need to explore, and I support it.

Preschool and school-aged children

Ultimately, we are planting seeds for children to be confident learners, successful students, engaged college students, and beyond. In the same vein, a preschooler may want to help wash dishes or build a structure in the living room. How we respond sends messages regarding how we, as parents, feel about the child's natural desire to have initiative. Should we react negatively, children learn to exile their natural abilities and develop strategies to avoid future shame, and ultimately, it may look like a lack of initiative, which is the opposite of what we want as they grow. This pattern continues into school-age children and beyond. As an educator and a committed learner, I know the importance of Self-led learning. When children are Self-led, they are more curious and confident, and they take risks and are willing to explore new things. They have persistence and will enjoy learning.

From an IFS perspective, humans' natural state is one of curiosity, confidence, and persistence, and when children are treated poorly, they take on burdens that cover these wonderful characteristics. Their parts take on beliefs that they are wrong for engaging in such pursuits and that they are bad, unworthy, and wrong for following their natural inclinations. In such examples, children learn to avoid getting hurt by exiling parts of themselves and develop protectors who avoid negative feedback. These protectors want to please, stay quiet, and become inner critics. So from this lens, Self-led parenting certainly reduces the number of burdens children may take on and allows children to follow their natural course of development.

Tweens and teens

As our children become tweens, teens, and young adults, they need more and more freedom to make their own choices. And, of course, we need to know they are responsible before they get certain freedoms. However, the challenge is: our growing children need to be able to practice making decisions to see how things work in the world and see what happens when they make bad decisions.

My daughter told me I should share with you why it's important to hold off on the quick "no!" She informed me that my parts would say no very quickly when she asked to do certain things. As she told me this, I sensed my part, who was fearful that something terrible would happen to her if I let her do some risky things in the world. When I led with this part, I made her feel trapped, and she shut down. She felt like I didn't trust her and value her opinions. If I could go back, I would have listened to her and then taken time to process with my parts before I responded.

Being a Self-led Parent is a Type of Leadership

When Self leads, our parts get what they need, and we treat others with respect and openness. Self-led parenting is a type of leadership at home. As leaders, parents support children to thrive, inspire them to try new things, and to develop shared family values. Good leadership makes it safe for children to be active contributors to the household. When we are taken over by our own manager parts, we tend to focus on the end goals, the product, rather than the process. "Get it done" is often the motto of parenting parts. We need to get there, finish this, be on time, make sure the kids do things and act a certain way. The problem is the manager parts tend to push, blame, coerce, shame, and apply undue pressure on our children. As a result, we may unknowingly create a home climate that feels unsafe. Corrections, exasperations, and demands tend to send shaming messages:

"You're not doing it right." "You are always late." "Why are you like this?" "Stop that and be more like this. . ." We think those messages will help our children change, yet more often, they communicate that they aren't good enough. Children will then often develop internal critics who take up the task of internal shaming to make the child do better to avoid external shame from parents. As a parent, you can ask, "Do I feel an agenda to get my child to become someone or something, or do I simply want to be with my child and feel curious about who they are and how I can support them on their path?"

Alfie Kohn, author of parenting books, shares that parents will say they want their children to be creative and innovative, to stand out among their peers with new and fresh ideas, and not to be a sheep following the herd; however, in real-time, the same parents tend to squash such behaviors with knee-jerk reactions. The message is: follow my rules, stay in control, don't talk back, and that's not how we do things. When children are compliant, and in line, parents show love, approval, and compliment their behavior. Yet, when they fall out of line, parents pull their love back, distance themselves, and show signs of disapproval. Thus, the ultimate message is: you do not deserve love unless you follow my rules, which consequently squelches the qualities parents want in their children (Kohn, 2005). Two of my clients found themselves in such a predicament. Here I will call them Joseph and William.

Client: Joseph

Joseph was raised in a home where children never talk back to their parents. If so, there would be harsh negative consequences. During a session, Joseph explained his shock that his daughter made demands, snapped back, and openly defied him. Joseph explained how he would never talk to his father as his daughter talks to him. He would be intimidated

81

by a look from his father and knew not to be disrespectful. Joseph told stories of how his daughter would "be disrespectful" in front of guests by not responding to them, or how she would barge out of her room demanding the music get turned down or get angry in the car if the music was too loud. Joseph's parts would be flabbergasted that she would act in such a way and often yelled back at her, demanded respect, or sent her back to her room. As parents, I think we can all resonate with Joseph's parts. I can recall speaking in anger when my children talked to me with disrespect.

As Joseph listened to his parts, one told him he wants her to be a good citizen, and when she acts like this, it feels worried he will look like a bad father. He found other parts who carry beliefs like: kids shouldn't talk back to their parents, or they will get in trouble. When Joseph was blended with these parts, he felt justified in snapping back, telling her that she may not speak to him this way. You may be thinking, so, what's the problem here? Children should talk respectfully to their parents. Although that may be true, how we get there matters. After Joseph worked with his parts, witnessed their stories, and helped them step out of the past situations where they were feeling judged and criticized by his father, a new world opened up to him. His parts began to allow Self to take the lead. Being more Self-led, Joseph was able to have curiosity about his daughter's reactions and started to wonder if she is sensitive to loud sounds. He noticed she has her own parts who were being reactive or shy around others. When he approached her from that space, she also settled down and was naturally more respectful and open to talking about what was happening. After spending time with his parts on his own, building relationships with them, he reported to me that "she's different"—meaning she wasn't so disrespectful.

Client: William

William, another client, sought me out for IFS parenting support because he found himself getting angry when his young children left their toys on the floor, got Play-Doh on the carpet, put their elbows on the table, and so on. He reported that he shamed his children, criticized them, and felt disgusted by their behavior. We got to know his parts who felt so upset. His parts showed him times in his life when he would get into trouble for similar behavior, especially with his stepfather. His stepfather criticized him for his behavior and even hit him for having his elbows on the table. His stepfather told William how he himself was beaten as a child and how good William has it. He threatened William that he could beat him to death if he wanted to. William found a vulnerable part that held shame, feeling that he was never enough and always wrong; even sitting at a table is wrong. His parents never gave reasons for how he should behave and assumed he should know why the rules were in place. Thus, when he got in trouble for putting his elbows on the table, his part said to him, "Why don't I know this?" William helped this part understand it wasn't his fault for the mistreatment, and consequently learned to be more patient with his children.

William also found a part that carried the belief that how you keep your house reflects your worth. This part showed William a time when he had a friend who lived in bad conditions, a dirty and unsanitary home. That friend was viewed negatively at school by his peers, and William's part associated having a dirty home with being shunned by others. After helping his parts feel seen, understood, and unburdened, he reported, "I've been more patient, less reactionary, more of a listener, and I could hold Self—not letting my parts talk." He began to see that what he once thought was bad behavior by his children was really their natural desire to explore. He found he could help them learn to clean up in a more patient way or have better table manners without inflicting the same type of shame that he received as a child.

•　　●　　•

There are times when we need to step in and make corrections. Yet, it's helpful to ask ourselves whether our children are doing things that actually hurt others, themselves, or the space in which we live, or is it our parts who are annoyed, threatened, or stressed. If it's the latter, it's better to pause and work with our parts before we speak. Richard Schwartz explains that parents' protector parts often exile children's excitement, freedom, and creativity if their protector parts feel threatened by those qualities. From my experience, the parents who squelch their children's freedom to express themselves were probably parented the same way. Their own natural abilities were exiled by their parents, and they developed protectors that kept those qualities away from the surface. Now, their managers, who have protected them so well growing up, continue the work and keep their own children in check. The work of Self-led parenting is to go inside and get to know our protector parts, their stories, and their jobs. We also find our exiles and witness and heal them so we parent in the present without the overlay of the past.

Getting to Know our Parts and our Children's Parts

Let's take time to get to know your own parts as well as your children's parts. Think about a challenging situation you've been having with your child or children. As you read this, pause as much as you need to listen to your parts and then move on to the next direction or question. Throughout this exercise, which is based on many of Richard Schwartz's teachings and IFS protocols, be sure to check that you are seeing things from your own eyes rather than seeing yourself there with the part or parts. If you see yourself, that's another part. Just like you can't see yourself without looking in a mirror, Self has the same perspective in our inner world.

EXERCISE

Get to Know Your Part

1. Think about a challenging situation between you and your child.

2. Notice first what happens in your body. Do you feel something in your stomach, your head, your shoulders, or your chest? Perhaps it's pressure, an ache, or tension. Send your breath to that area of your body and let it know you are here, ready to listen.

3. Ask that area of your body: what do you want me to know? You may see a scene, hear a voice, or get more of a feeling or sensation. As this is happening, you're starting to get to know a part.

4. Take a moment to see how you feel toward that part. If you don't feel open, curious, or compassionate, there is probably another part here. Ask that part if it's willing to give you just enough space so you can be here. For instance, you may find yourself saying, "Yes, I hate that

too!" That is another part. Self is more open and patient, curious and compassionate.

5. If you find yourself thinking about this part or about what it shows you, perhaps notice if your attention is in your head or your heart. If it's in your head with a lot of thinking or analyzing, you are blending with a cognitive part. You can ask that part to relax back, perhaps take notes, so you can hear the part's story. Now, see if you can drop your attention down to your heart as if you can see through a lens in your heart area. It will feel softer and more spacious.

6. Once you are back with the original part you want to get to know, ask it to share what it wants you to know, see, or have you feel. This is a part who needs your loving attention and understanding. Even if it says harsh words about your children, know that it is doing its best to help you in some way. Perhaps you can share back on how what it is saying makes sense; of course, it is overloaded, frustrated, or hurt.

7. Ask the part if it is trying to help you in some way. If it is, ask how it's trying to help and what it's concerned will happen if it doesn't do its job. A frustrated part may say, "I'm trying to keep the kids on track and keep the house from falling apart." If the part doesn't have a job and it is just sad or hurt, be there for it and let it tell you its story.

8. Ask the part how old it thinks you are. Parts often think you are younger than you are, as they often take on their jobs when you were young and not able to change your living situation. Update the part if it thinks you are younger and tell it about yourself, perhaps things that

you feel proud about, your abilities and strengths. Notice how it reacts to this news.

9. Now ask the part what it needs from you and see if it would like help with its job or if it doesn't have a job, perhaps it needs some care from you, a hug, holding hands, or more listening. Negotiate what you can do moving forward with your child/ren if the part is willing to give you space.

Perhaps stop here if this feels complete or enough for now. If you wish to continue, the next steps are below. This part of the exercise is a unique technique that I have stumbled upon. I have learned through practice and experimentation that we can hear from our children's parts, just like we can hear from our own. Most of the time, it's better to have children tell us about their parts, yet this exercise has brought me and many others clarity over the years. When I did this exercise, my children's parts seemed to let me know how my corrections or frustration made them feel shamed and unloved. They shared how they had to push me away, or they would feel the shame underneath. Knowing that, my parts allowed me, Self, to help, as opposed to feeling rejected, hurt, and angry when my children's parts came up. My parts also didn't want my children to feel unloved or shamed. So I became more patient and took the time to observe my children, seeking understanding, before I responded. Again, in response, they were more patient, helpful, and willing to take guidance. Here is the next part of the exercise.

EXERCISE

Get to Know Your Child's Part

1. Check again to see how open, curious, and compassion-ate you feel. If not, ask any part present if they would be willing to give you enough space to do this next piece.

2. When you feel open, imagine your child in whatever scene makes sense. Perhaps it's the same one above that caused you discomfort.

3. Then notice how your child is reacting to you. Take it in. Are they rolling their eyes? Deflated? Angry? Avoidant? Again, stay open and curious. Notice this is a part of them!

4. Ask with true compassionate openness why they have to respond this way. What would happen if they didn't protect themselves this way? Often, we hear they would feel hurt or unloved if these protectors didn't do their job.

5. Ask the part what it would rather have you, the parent, do in these situations. How do they want you to act? What would you say or do? The message often seems clear, wise, and touching.

6. What else does this one want to tell you regarding what you can do moving forward to help the child?

7. If it feels right, send some love to the part of your child who can get hurt if this protector doesn't do its job.

In addition to exercises such as these, we can help our children get to know their own parts, and we can learn about them, as well, through inquiry. Ideally, our children should be the ones telling us about their parts, so we don't assume how they feel. When they are upset or acting in a way that triggers your parts, take a deep breath and pause. Tell yourself, "This is a part I am seeing, not my child's Self," and get curious about that part. Ask the child questions as if you were approaching one of your own parts with the same compassionate openness. You may ask, "Can you tell me what you are feeling right now?" After the child talks, you may say, "I see that you are frustrated; that's ok. Can you tell me why?" As they talk, you can say, "Oh, that makes sense why that part of you feels that way. Do you want to say more?" We are normalizing that we all have parts. Over time, we can say things like, "Do you notice that one part of you feels that way (mad at a friend) and another doesn't (still wants to be friends)? What does the part who wants to be friends want to say?" You can follow up with, "Ah, that makes sense to me. You have one part who is hurt and another who is angry, and all along, there is another who just wants to be friends again. Does that make sense to you?" As children get older and more comfortable talking about their parts, you can ask them to "go inside and ask the part what it wants you to know or show you."

Children often like to externalize their parts. For instance, they can draw them, pretend their toys or action figures are their parts, or pretend anything is their part, like a stone or an item in the room. They can act out their parts through these materials. A toy dog could be their worried part, or a dragon could be their angry part. They can even talk to the part directly. "What do you want to say to your worried doggy?" you might ask. Often children drop into Self and say the most insightful and profound things. We can also talk directly to their parts. "Is it ok if I talk to the worried doggy?" You might share how you understand the worry and help reassure the part of how you are also going to be there to support and help your child.

Once, when my son was in Kindergarten, and his mom and I just separated during our divorce, he needed a permission slip signed for a school field trip. It required both parents' signatures

(I had a part who was not happy about that). My son was concerned because he didn't think his mom would be able to sign it in time, since he was with me that week. I tried to reassure him that I would get her to sign it, but he started to spiral, and usually, once he got upset, it took a while to help him calm down. I then walked him over to a toy called the You-niverse, created by David Cantor, which looks like a solar system with a large yellow sphere in the middle that represents Self and metal wire rings around it. There are smaller balls of many colors that represent our parts, and you place those on the wire rings. My children and I decided that the closer the ball is to the yellow ball in the center, Self, the stronger we feel that part. So, when I took him to the You-niverse, I asked him to pick out a ball from a wooden bowl that represents his worry about getting the permission slip signed. He picked a ball and put it as close as possible to the big yellow ball in the center (Self). "Ok," I said, "that part feels a lot of worry, and it feels like it's really close to you." He nodded his little face. I said, "Can I talk to that part?" He nodded again. I said, "I promise I will get Mom to sign the form, and it is my job to make that happen. I won't forget. You can give that job to me." He took a deep breath, moved the ball far back to the outer rings, and I saw his body relax. On one knee, I gave him a deep hug. "Are you ready to go to school?" I asked. He nodded and picked up his backpack, and walked into the kitchen. Once there, he dropped his backpack and sprinted back to the You-niverse. I leaned into the doorway just in time to see him take the ball off the rings and put it in the bowl. I thought to myself, "Wow, he really let it go." That moment taught me the power of IFS and Self-led parenting.

The Power of Repair

During our reflections of the day, we often realize we were taken over by our parts and said or did things we didn't mean. Engaging in repair is a powerful way to regain connection with our children and avoid the creation of burdens. Oftentimes, children take on negative beliefs about themselves when parents say or do hurtful things. They may feel unloved, unworthy, or that they are bad and it's their fault. Left alone, the message is clear. We meant what we said.

I used to have parts who believed that since I was the parent, I was allowed to say or do what I wanted. That was an abuse of power. Just because I have the physical ability to help create or adopt a child, I do not have the right to treat other humans disrespectfully or in hurtful ways. IFS helped me realize I was taken over by parts when I yelled, showed disappointment, or withdrew my love. I started to go back to my children and tell them about my parts, how I was taken over by a part who was angry, and it wasn't their fault that I snapped at them. Usually, my children are very open to sincere apologies, and their protectors relax and allow them to feel and show a connection with me. Of course, after repeated offenses and apologies, children's protectors learn apologies don't mean much, so we do have to help our parts let us lead. But in the meantime, take the time to apologize without telling them what they should or shouldn't have done. That can be a later discussion, if it's necessary. When we don't apologize, it sends the message that we truly believe what we said, we don't care, we disapprove of them, and there really is something wrong with them. Repair can help reduce the amount of burdens children take on.

Get Started: Take Note of Your Parts

One of the easiest ways to be Self-led is to take stock of what parts are present as we parent. Again, you will sense if you are in Self or blended with a part just by pausing and looking inside. You may sense you have an agenda, a sense of urgency, or pressure to get a certain and often highly specific outcome. If so, ask:

"Who's here?" If you get a response, begin listening and witnessing what this part wants to share with you. If you don't get a response, take a few deep breaths, ask your mind to relax, and breathe your heart bigger. The key is that you are listening, feeling, and watching, rather than thinking or figuring it out. When you feel curious and compassionate, ask your parts questions until you feel like you understand, and then let them know what and how you understand what they are feeling. If a part is trying to push things along, get the kids to bed, or even make you lay on the couch and cover yourself with a blanket for ten minutes, it's trying to help you. Know that, and approach it from that place. All of your protectors, no matter how extreme, want to help you, save you, and shield you from feeling the pain held by the vulnerable parts of you. So, when you want to push your child to do their chores or brush their teeth, and it feels stressful, pause and notice what part is leading. Get to know the part and build a relationship with it. It needs to be seen and understood by you before it lets you take the lead.

Remember the parts you find; perhaps write them down or make a parts map. Continue to go back to them. When they trust you, they will let you lead. They've been doing their job for a long time, perhaps your whole life. It may take time to trust you. The next time you are having some uneasiness with your child, pause and answer these questions:

HELPFUL GUIDE

Tracking My Parenting Parts

1. *When my child just said that, did that, or didn't respond, what was my automatic reaction or impulse?*

This is the first part to get to know. If it felt like a dragon about to rear its fiery breath, an arrow that wants to fly out of your mouth, or an immediate shutdown and numbing feeling—that is a part trying to help remedy the situation in some way.

2. *What happened next? Did you react from that first part? If so, what did you say or do?* Observe how that part reacted, and notice the reaction of the child.

3. *If you didn't react from the first part, what shift did you make? What was the other thought or impulse?*
Notice if this was another part reacting to the first one. Perhaps it's a responsible part who says, "We can't blow fire at this child!" See, parts are helpful. However, ask that part about its job. I bet it's not very happy having to be the responsible one. You can ask, "What's it like doing your job?" and "What do you think might happen if you didn't do it or if you stopped? The answers will reveal their fears and probably how exhausting it is to have this role.

4. *What other points of view are going through your mind?* Perhaps, you are thinking. "My kids have to follow the rules!" or "Perhaps I should just let them do what they want." All of these thoughts could be other parts tossing in their two cents. How do we know? Do a litmus test: Am I curious or compassionate? Do I have an agenda? How is my child reacting to me? Am I more in my head or my heart?

5. As Richard Schwartz often says, once you are curious and open, "Notice who is listening to your parts. It's you, Self," You are the caregiver, coach, conductor, and ultimate compassionate and trustworthy leader of your

parts. Over time, they will learn to trust you. Ask them, "Is it ok if I help or if I take the lead on this one?" Perhaps the parts want to share with you their concerns and fears first. Reassure them and ask their permission to give you just enough space to be with your child, so you can help guide them in a healthy way. The parts are usually quite amazed at how Self can parent with ease and grace.

Setting Limits from a Self-led Place

Being Self-led does not mean we are permissive parents. Setting limits and boundaries for children are acts of love when they are done with compassion and understanding. Children may not like being told "no," and Self-led parenting doesn't always avoid pain or suffering. But we can hold space for them as they process the "no." It's one of the hardest things about parenting, but it can be beautiful if we can stay compassionate through the limits or boundaries.

Dr. Montessori said we should follow the child, but we don't follow them off a cliff. Proper limits are healthy and help children manage this life. Dr. Montessori explained that a child is like a river, and our limits are the banks of the river. The banks give the river its riverness; without them, the river does not exist. However, how the banks reside is crucial. If the banks are too wide, the river loses itself and becomes a swamp. So true with permissive parenting. When children have no limits, they lack direction and may feel unsafe. Limits indirectly show children how much we care about them and their safety.

On the other hand, when the banks of the river are too narrow, the river starts to quicken and often rages or overflows the banks. So true for children of authoritarian parents. Children living under overly strict rules may misbehave more at school as an outlet, or they punish others around them the way they are being punished at home. So for each child, we must adjust our limits to help the child have a healthy life course. Our limits are created by observing our children and determining what limits need to be in place.

The composition of river banks matter. If our limits are made of sand, they become eroded. If they are more firm, we can hold healthy limits. That being said, how we hold limits matters. When Self-led, we can say "no" in a good way, showing our love and care and being present if the child is upset. You can say, "I can see you really want to do that, and I'm sorry, that's not one of the choices right now." Remember, the key is to know if you, Self, are setting a limit, feeling loving, calm, and confident, or if it is a part with an agenda and often with a negative vibe.

When parts are in the lead, they often set limits that are not necessary. Perhaps they create rules that their parents imposed or ones based on fear. Our parts are trying to help us, and they are self-serving. Our parts may react because we need rest or because we are overwhelmed. I ask myself this question: "Is my child's behavior bothering me, or am I just bothered?" This is an indirect way of saying, "Am I blended with a part that just wants to be left alone and wants peace and quiet?" If so, we can tell our children about those parts, speaking for them. We might say, "I notice a part of me is getting overwhelmed by the noise. Can we turn down the volume a bit?" And then go find a way to be with those parts.

One great thing about being "in Self": wisdom comes naturally. We cannot always follow specific parenting advice from books or websites because humans are not machines who react the same to certain adjustments. If you open your heart and truly see your child, you will know what to do. Here are some questions you can ask yourself if you are wondering if you are parenting in a healthy way.

HELPFUL GUIDE

How am I Parenting?

1. Do I treat my child with respect and dignity?

2. Do I feel an agenda most of the time I am interacting with my child?

3. Does my child often react negatively to me?

4. Where did I learn the rules I enforce, and what do I think would happen if I didn't enforce them? If the result seems dire, there's a good chance there is a part there to get to know. We often parent from fear that our parts hold. Our parts have learned that some rules keep you safe and may still be reacting to your childhood conditions rather than the current ones.

5. Do I feel positive or negative after interacting with my child?

You may find that your parts feel the need to create specific limits based on past situations or fears, and sadly, our children don't get to experience the authentic version of us when we parent from parts. It feels like a disconnection, like we are in the same room, but not really there. Children want to feel our presence and our authentic Self. When you parent from a Self-led place, children tend to be more helpful and even compliant because their protectors are less likely to be up.

Routines are Life

We may think that the sit-down talks, the celebrations, and the family dinners are the crucial parenting moments. Those are truly important moments, but they take up a small percentage of the actual time we spend with our children. The daily routines—getting out the door, getting school work done, getting showered, and brushing teeth take up a huge amount of time. During those times, we are interacting with our children, and we often have one goal—get it done. With that agenda in the forefront, we often push through routines, and they are often parts led. We get bossy and frustrated. Try allowing for more time to be in the routines. See what happens if you ask your parts to give you space so you can be the one to be with your child during these times. The additive effect of positive interactions during routines will do wonders for your relationship with your child. Just think how many times you have finally made it into the car and are driving somewhere when you are ready to have a conversation with your child, and they put up walls or barely respond. Their reaction is a result of the moments before when we plowed over them or said things that were shaming in order to get out the door.

HELPFUL GUIDE

Routines: Questions to ask yourself

1. How can we arrange our schedule differently to allow for more time for transitions?

2. What are things that trigger my parts during routines? Find those parts and get to know them.

3. How often does my own stress overflow on my child as we are trying to get out the door? How do my parts feel when someone treats me that way?

4. What is my biggest fear if our routines don't go well? What messages do I hear inside? Allow those messages to be trailheads for your exploration of your parts.

HELPFUL GUIDE

Review: So What Do We Do?

1. Get to know your parts who come up while parenting, perhaps with an IFS Practitioner or Therapist. Once you understand them, show your understanding and appreciate their intent. Perhaps ask if they are willing to take on a new job or if they would be willing to let you take the lead with your child.

2. Check-in with those parts often to see how they are doing/feeling.

3. While parenting, notice when these parts start to take over and ask them to step back and let you take the lead. If they seem reluctant, listen to their concerns. If necessary, speak for the parts.

4. Notice your child has parts, too, and a part may be taking over when they are "misbehaving." Their part may be reactive. Remind yourself that this is a part, and there is a need underneath—perhaps to be seen or heard. The part reacting is not the child's true Self.

5. Thank your parts for letting you take the lead, for trusting you, and for giving you space to be with your child.

6. When you parent, talk for your parts, not from them. As you listen to your parts, you can tell your children how they feel. If your part is angry, instead of letting it take you over and use your mouth and body, ask it to tell you what's happening and then say to your child something like, "I have a part that is feeling angry because it really doesn't like it when you ignore me."

7. When you feel successful being present with your child, ask your parts how they feel now that you had such a positive interaction with your child.

Here are other examples of talking for your parts as a parent and doing repairs:

HELPFUL GUIDE

Examples of talking for your parts

1. "I have a frustrated part that thinks we are going to be late."

2. "When you said that to me, I felt a part inside who felt hurt."

3. "I have a part who wants to yell right now, but I'm sitting with it."

4. "I have a part who wants to help you with everything because that is what this part thinks it means to be a good parent. I'm sorry I took over what you were doing."

5. "When I yelled at you earlier, I was taken over by a frustrated part that really needed some downtime. I shouldn't have let that part yell at you; I'm sorry."

6. "I have a part that worries about your safety, and I know when that part takes over, I can really make you feel trapped."

Key Takeaways and Helpful Nuggets

Parts beget parts. When we are regulated, our children can be regulated as well. They respond in kind. When children react negatively to us, if we do a You-turn, we will see that we almost always were acting from a part, and that is what the child is responding to. As we return to Self, they can too.

When we parent, we are often blended with managers, and even kindly spoken messages tend to have an agenda. We have to be aware of agendas like: my child has to change and be different.

Children experience this as shame and feel like they are not enough or too much, even with micro corrections. It's important to remember to be curious about your children and their parts, giving the message that they are loved just as they are, even during stressful routines when we have to get things done. It's important for children to know that it is normal and healthy to have needs and to express them.

Corrections can happen and are necessary at times. It's important to know that guidance is most effective when we are as Self-led as possible. When we appreciate how our children are different from us, with different approaches to things, and we celebrate that, children can handle corrections and discipline more easily.

As children become blended with parts, we can help name them. "I see that a part of you is frustrated; is that right?" We can listen to what their parts are feeling without correcting and teaching, and then share back what we understand. If we sit with our children with a loving heart while they are blended with their parts like we would sit with our own, they will feel seen and heard, and then their parts can soften.

Above all, as we get to know our own parts and learn to care for them, we can turn to our children with that same love (Schwartz, 2021).

Self-led Spirituality

IFS IS NOT TOUTED as a spiritual practice. However, IFS feels spiritual or meditative to many, since we often close our eyes and go inside to explore our inner worlds. When we uncover our Self Energy, we feel connected to others, to the planet, and to the universe. We often experience something bigger than ourselves and connect with our ancestral lineage while we are healing our parts.

What I share here comes from years of observations from my own IFS process, witnessing my client's experiences, and from listening to many people's IFS stories. IFS helps us find our higher Self, and in that space, we tend to find what we seek while engaging in spiritual practices: peace, tranquility, healing, wisdom, and connection to something greater than us. Thus, I feel IFS can help you reach your spiritual intentions, no matter the spiritual practice in which you participate.

From my personal experience, and based on the work I do with people every day, contentment seems to emerge when we return to the natural, birthright qualities of our true Selves. Our natural qualities include connectedness, curiosity, compassion, creativity, playfulness, and the capacity to feel joy. I believe we are all born with a light inside, connected to G-d, nature, Source, the Universe, or to life itself. That light, Self Energy, carries and supports our freedom to express who we are. Many people report seeing a golden or white light when they see Self Energy, and many spiritual traditions refer to such light as a healing or divine source. I believe this light supports our ability to flourish if it is allowed to shine unencumbered.

Yet life seems to carry hurtful experiences that dim or almost extinguish our light, sometimes beginning in infancy. On the other hand, when children receive unconditional love, and people around them value what they bring, their uniqueness of expression and thought, they don't take on beliefs like their light is too much or insufficient. They can shine with joy and perhaps carry that into adulthood.

Self Energy Cannot be Lost

In IFS, we believe Self cannot be destroyed or harmed in any way. We are born with Self Energy, which cannot be used up or lost. Self Energy is a never-ending source. Richard Schwartz compares Self Energy to a magical kitchen (Schwartz, 2008), where the refrigerator keeps refilling every time we open it.

We don't feel Self Energy when we are blended with our parts, so we unblend to access it. Our parts feel fear and emotional pain, and we experience all that along with them when we are blended. And yet, when they step back a bit and give us space, the Self Energy is right there. They have more access to us (Self), and we can be with our parts who can carry so much pain.

All of our Self Energy is of the same quality, mine, yours, Richard Schwartz's, everyone's. Self Energy is Self Energy, and we are all connected through it. Self Energy is like water. We all have water in our bodies, and it's all the same. We all have Self Energy, and no one's Self Energy is different from anyone else's. With practice, we all can access it.

Paintings and other images of religious or spiritual figures often depict them surrounded by white or golden light. They have a halo or an aura. These images seem universal. We instinctively recognize that light as something special, divine, mystical, or holy. Some people are able to see people's auras, various colors that relate to our chakras, the colors of the rainbow, starting with red in your lower chakra. You may have a green aura if you are heart-centered, for instance. Years ago, I had an epiphany. I was curious why Jesus was often displayed with a white or golden light around him or simply a halo. Then I thought, if it is true that the divine came into a human form, then, of course, the aura would be white light, the perfect balance of all the chakras. When we shine light through a prism, we see the rainbow; the light holds all these colors. So it makes sense that enlightened people would be balanced and give off a white or golden light.

In IFS, we believe Self is inside of us, connected to all of life, and when our parts take over our consciousness, we don't experience the qualities of Self in those moments. By being with our parts, who are so desperately trying to help us feel ok, we can help them trust us and let our light shine. We feel more present when our parts soften back and trust us to stand in our place or sit in our seats without protective measures in full activation.

IFS and Religion and Spirituality

I remember having a crucible moment while reading the book Being Peace by Thich Nhat Hahn. He taught us that in order to make a difference in the world, we have to go within and find our own peace and lead with that. He also shared that the practice of Zen Buddhism can be applied to any practice or religion. For instance, Zen Buddhism teaches us to be present. I remember Thich Nhat Hahn giving the example of washing dishes. If we are thinking about the rest of our day or what we wish we were doing instead of washing dishes, washing dishes feels like a chore. However, if we stay present, in the moment, we may enjoy the motions of washing dishes, find an interesting or efficient process, or simply enjoy the bubbles and the tactile experience. I propose here that IFS can also be applied the same way, to all aspects of our lives, and to our spirituality.

If you are religious, imagine a time when you prayed and were keenly present. Perhaps you felt a divine connection. If you are not religious and have a spiritual practice, you have probably noticed the same thing; when we are present and fully engaged in our practice, something deep happens. When I was young, I attended a Jewish summer camp. They taught us about *kavanah*, praying from our hearts, and fully being there in the moment. During those times, I noticed I could have a personal connection with what feels Divine. I realize now, in those moments of deep connection, I was in Self.

Following that line of thought, it seems that if you follow any sacred or indigenous traditions, being in Self while you do your practice would allow you to connect to all you seek. Oftentimes, prayer, meditation, and rituals can become monotonous, or we may blend with a part who feels obliged to engage in such traditions. In those moments, we often go through the motions, and our heart is not present. We may feel bored or anxious about other life demands waiting in the wings. If you can ask those parts to give you just enough space for you to be here, for you to be the one engaged in this ritual, you will find a deeper connection to your prayers or practice. Our mind, body, and spirit converge, acting in harmony, and our parts sense it and relax.

Perhaps you have had bad experiences growing up in your spiritual traditions or religion. You may have felt let down or abandoned by G-d. If so, it makes sense that you would have protector parts who shy away, angry parts who resist, or dissociative parts who make you sleepy when you try to engage in rituals. If you want to engage more deeply, it is important to tend to those parts and form relationships with them. You may find a younger version of yourself still in the past, experiencing hardships, dominance, and, oftentimes, abuse. You can witness those parts, let them tell you or show you their story, and then retrieve them to the present. If the part needs a redo or needs you to stand up to someone, that can happen, too. Deep in our hearts, I believe we all know humans make religion bad, painful, or use it to abuse power over others, and true spirituality and religion is about love and caring for others and the planet. So personally, I protect my parts and make sure I only enter safe spaces for spiritual practice.

Spirituality During IFS Sessions

I have witnessed people connect to religious entities during IFS sessions, and I have in my own sessions as well. As parts have been unburdened, people have reported Jesus, Mary Magdalene, Quan Yin, ArchAngel Michael, and others have come to assist. Other people have witnessed angels, spirit guides, and power animals. All of these figures seem to carry qualities of Self, especially compassion, courage, wisdom, and perspective. People then form relationships with these compassionate guides who offer comfort to parts and to the Self. I have also witnessed people meet their ancestors and others who have passed; they enter the scene while healing or when called on in order to have a connection, repair, or to say the things we wish we would have said before they died.

It seems like these figures, who we call Guides in IFS, come in ways people can understand. I studied education for a large part of my life, and one of the main principles of teaching is to meet students where they are based on their prior knowledge. New knowledge is like a Lego block, and it needs to nest on another. Without the proper experiences or prior knowledge, it's like trying to stick a Lego block to glass. In the same way, I believe the Source of things has come to people on this earth in ways we can understand. Different religions have different religious figures, all from the same Source. In the same vein, when people are in Self and open to a deeper connection, they can witness mystical things in a way that makes sense for them. Self has no ego, and neither do the compassionate beings who show up for us. I feel our guides are intermediaries between us and G-d; they embody Self Energy and are here to help us. When my guides are with me, I feel an increase in Self Energy as my parts relax and give me more access to my Self.

Being Your Own Guru

From my experience, when we are in Self, we tap into higher wisdom. When we are Self-led, we think more clearly and have a keen perspective. But there is more; we have access to the wisdom of Self Energy. We seem to get downloads of truth and knowledge regarding what we should do next. Although I have utmost respect for having spiritual teachers, when we trust in the wisdom that comes through, we can be our own guru and receive answers to our deeper existential questions.

In IFS, we believe that we can reach Self when parts are willing to step back and give us space. The worry relaxes, the fear subsides, the intensity settles, and the overwhelm soothes. And there, Self is. In addition, we also have the capability to drop into Self using various techniques. When we do so, I have noticed our parts witness Self's presence and then step back as a result. It's as if they see their trusted leader and now feel safe without the need to protect and run the system.

There are various techniques people use to "drop into Self." It feels like a dropping sensation to many. For me, my center of attention moves from my head to my heart. Other techniques I have used include visualizing a ball of Self Energy in my chest, golden light radiating to my parts. I have also visualized my parts standing in a circle around me, me sending them Self Energy, and while they receive it, they send their own back to me. This visualization looks akin to a Tesla ball.

We assume parts have their own Self Energy, and they even have their own parts. This may seem hard to imagine. It helps me to think of my parts as younger versions of myself who either were exiled or took on protective roles. If that is true, of course, they have their own parts! My 11-year-old part, who watched my parents fight, already had parts at that time and might have developed more during those horrible experiences. So now, when I go to that 11-year-old, he is there with all of his parts. He also had his own Self Energy at that time, so he still does. Helping parts eventually see their own Self Energy has been very transformational for people's healing process. If you like, try the meditation of asking your parts to stand in a circle around you. Share your light/Self Energy with them, and then see if they can also send their Self Energy back to you.

If that doesn't resonate with you and if you tend to sense parts in your body, you can try the exercise that follows:

EXERCISE

Points of Light

1. Parts often seem to reside in different areas of our body. So when you feel settled, curious, compassionate, a threshold of Self Energy, start scanning your body, noticing your parts.

2. Remember, they have their own Self Energy. If possible, start to see their Self Energy as golden balls or points of

---

light, and then notice those points all over your body, like a starry night sky.

3. Take time to feel the expansiveness that settles in, noticing that healing light inside of you, the light that has existed since the very first light was sparked. You are truly connected to the whole universe through that light, and so are your parts.

Head to Heart

Recently, I have found a very simple technique for dropping into Self. I call it *head to heart*. Start by noticing how much activity is happening in your mind, all the activity above your shoulders. Usually, I find that mental activity is my intellectual, analytical, worried, striving, and other cognitive parts. Now, simply allow your attention and your focus to drop into your heart space, like an elevator going down, and notice how it feels when you try to see through your heart's lens.

When doing so, you can feel your Self Energy grow, your body ease, and your parts relax. It is as if they were children on a playground who were moments before having an argument, feeling disrupted and alone, and then the trusted teacher emerges, and their systems relax, knowing they are safe. When you drop into this place, you can often see or feel your parts more clearly.

Spiritual Bypass

A word of caution here: beware of spiritual bypass. Spiritual bypass happens when we use meditation or other spiritual practices to block, ignore, or exile our parts. We may find a temporary sense of ease or expansiveness through various spiritual practices, but we should ensure that we are not ignoring our parts or somehow blocking them from our consciousness. I have met many people who have had deep spiritual practices for years before they found IFS. After doing IFS, they realized that although their practice had given them many skills, they were not healing the parts who really needed attention. On the positive side, their prior practices do enable them to go deeply into Self while doing IFS, oftentimes. People also found they were doing their practice from a Self-like, spiritual part or a spiritual seeker part. To be clear, I am not suggesting that any spiritual practice does not have merit; I'm suggesting that you look inside and see who is practicing, praying, sitting, meditating, or doing a specific ritual. Is it a part? You will know if you have a self-serving agenda rather than a clear purpose or intention. I have had and still have spiritual parts, and as I look back, I can see when I was in Self in my various spiritual practices and when my parts with agendas were in the lead.

When I was parts-led, I often felt desperation for healing, superstition (fear), and even a deep longing for connection with my ancestors. When I was 17 years old, I started dabbling in metaphysics, and I remember times when I was scared to leave the house without my special stones and crystals. I would hold certain stones and seemed to find some peace from my worries. I see now that I had a part that helped soothe my worries this way, but I did not heal my worried part until I found IFS. And yet, there were a number of times in my life when I felt I received clear messages and downloads on how to use such stones when I was more in Self. I had experiences where it was abundantly clear and immediate that the stones helped with healing.

In other instances, I was invited to join sacred ceremonies, like a sweat lodge. During my first sweat, I felt completely open, curious, humble, and loved ones who had passed came to me during the ceremony. However, at other times, I had parts who thought I was on "a special" spiritual path and was an evolved human. During those sweats, I found myself on the ground, in agony from the heat. I eventually stopped doing sweats. I started to feel uneasy about engaging in Native American sacred spiritual traditions. I felt like I was taking something that wasn't my own and engaging in cultural appropriation.

We all have Self-like parts who want to do good, who may be spiritual, and who may help us feel like we are on an enlightened path. Although they have good intentions, upon closer observation, we find they always have other self-serving agendas. The agenda may be to seek healing, wisdom, or even power. Yet with all parts-led activities, there are usually unintended consequences. We may feel like we are searching with no end in sight or somehow realize that others are pulling away from us when we talk about our spiritual journeys.

Wisdom In Self Energy

Little did we know that Self was always right there, and when we notice our parts with an open heart, we have arrived. Self is the one noticing. Self carries those qualities we seek: wisdom, clarity, calmness, compassion, and courage. When we sit in that place, we can connect to higher things and to the enormity of the universe. Richard Schwartz has explained that Self is like a particle and a wave (Schwartz and Sweezy, 2020). In our wave state, we sense how we are connected to all things, to each other; there is no separateness. It may feel like what the Buddhists call "no-Self" (we lose our ego). And in the particle state, we realize we are also an individual, with our own experiences and personalities in Self, with our parts; we are Self-led, Self in action (Schwartz, 2021). In Self, we realize that true spirituality is not about us. It's not about me. Things come through us for the betterment of all. Self can be the Guru our parts seek, and the wisdom of the universe is right there, inside of us, inside of Self Energy we all share.

In the words of J. Krishnamurti:

> In oneself lies the whole world, and if you know
> how to look and learn, then the door is there,
> and the key is in your hand. Nobody on earth
> can give you either that key or the door to open,
> except Yourself.
>
> Excerpt from a talk at Stanford University
> *In You Are The World*, Published in 1972

Is this Natural?

To some, this chapter may or may not resonate with you or may create fear of the supernatural. That makes sense if your parts have learned to fear these things or to believe in one particular way of thinking. I'd like to propose here that what feels supernatural might actually feel *natural* if our senses were more acute and we had full access to what our brains are capable of. IFS is a good example of this evolution. Years ago, we may have thought talking to our parts was something people did who were delusional, yet now, as people around the world use IFS in their daily practice, it has become a "normal" way to exist in the world. I hope one day, we are all comfortable with what feels supernatural now and discover that spirituality is a natural part of our existence.

Spiritual Exercise

There was a time during the COVID pandemic when I attended a Zoom prayer service from home. We were at the place in the service where we could pray silently and connect with G-d in a way that felt right to us. In the past, I normally had asked for things like health for my family or for certain successes. In that moment, I realized that a part of me asks for those things, a part who is scared of losing people and who wants status. I asked that part to step back and went deep into my heart. Then I knew what to do; I asked G-d, "What do you want me to know?" I heard a loving voice say to me, "You don't need acceptance from others; you have mine." That was the first time I felt what it was like to be held by something greater than me. I (my Self) felt like a part, being held by a Larger Self—G-d. Then I realized: I am the Self for my parts, and I can be held lovingly by G-d. With that holding, I can hold my parts with the same divine love. Prior to that moment, I only sensed G-d as a source of judgment and an advisor for doing good things. Being held this way has relaxed my whole system because my parts feel even safer letting me be with them, knowing this other force is with us.

Here I offer you one more exercise you can try as you begin a spiritual ritual or prayer:

EXERCISE

Deepening Your Spiritual Practice: Receiving Messages

1. Sit in a comfortable position and take some cleansing breaths. Notice how your body feels in your seat, and how you are connected to the ground.

2. Notice how much activity is in your head, above your shoulders, and let your attention drop into your heart area as if your heart could see with its own inner lens. If that is difficult, ask any parts in your mind if they are willing to sit next to you and watch you be here; perhaps they can take notes so they can make connections and debrief with you afterward.

3. Be still; be still on the inside. Let your heart and Self Energy expand wider, offering a soothing calmness to all

---

your parts. Notice how much Self Energy you feel, perhaps as a percentage or as a band of energy, and then as you breathe, expand that energy wider. Notice you can even fill the room with your Self Energy with practice.

4. When you feel a concentration of Self Energy (it's ok if that takes time and a number of sitting practices), set an intention for your prayer or ritual.

5. Open your receptivity by relaxing into no thought. Watch, wait, and listen like you would a film.

6. If you are praying to a presence, wait for the presence to be felt. Sit with the essence. Allow your heart to guide you. Feel what it is like to simply be with this presence or essence, and when it feels right, you may offer your prayers, your thanks, or even ask if there is a message it wants to give you, something it wants you to see or understand.

7. Spend as much time here as feels right; be humble, knowing this isn't really about you. You are allowing yourself to be an opening, a portal to help you create more healing in the world.

8. Offer any gratitude or thanks that feels natural.

9. Afterward, it may help to check in with your parts and see how they experienced this meditation. You may find one who is skeptical, scared, worried, or even guilty if what you did goes against some of the lessons you learned growing up. If so, sit with these parts and listen to them, and if possible, offer them your compassion, understanding, and Self Energy. Comfort them the way you always needed to be comforted.

Final words

ALTHOUGH IFS is used in clinical, coaching, and educational settings, I think it's fair to say that IFS can also be a way of life. It certainly has become that for me. My parenting, marriage, work, and friendships have improved since I found IFS. Whenever I'm in a conflict, I try to take a You-turn and see what's happening in my body, and what parts need my attention. I've learned to notice when I'm blended with a part, and I have created good relationships with my parts. It brings me hope knowing that when I am Self-led, life's troubles smooth out naturally.

IFS is not the end all, be all. In order to find peace and good health, we need to take care of our physical bodies, the spaces in which we live, and for many—our spirituality. When those areas are lacking, it is harder to be Self-led because those areas affect our parts. When we don't eat well, we may feel sluggish or anxious. If our bodies are in pain from lack of care, many different parts could be activated, such as feeling down, frustrated, or hopeless. When our homes or workspaces are overly disorganized, we often feel disorderly inside. That being said, IFS can improve your life greatly, even if those areas of your life are not in order. Personally, I found self-improvement has parallel paths, and being with our parts gives us more availability for eating well, taking care of our bodies, finding spirituality, and making our living and work spaces conducive to good health. Being with our parts helps us move into the self-care space, and self-care improves our ability to be with our parts. IFS can help improve our relationships with ourselves and our overall health.

One of the greatest gifts IFS has given me is the reduction of fear and worry. What would it be like if we didn't live in fear? We could walk in awareness with confidence and courage. We could know that we can make mistakes and have the ability to find solutions to move forward. We could take healthy risks and live life more fully. Living with fear is moving through life with our scared younger parts exposed, making life decisions for us, our protectors running the show, and avoiding pain and discomfort.

Richard Schwartz shares that only our parts hold fear. Self cannot be harmed. Self-led living creates awareness, and we can draw upon the strength and courage of Self Energy to be with our parts who hold fear. Without fear, we still see real danger and can hopefully avoid it, but that's different from living in the sometimes crippling fear of what could happen. At times, when nothing dangerous is physically happening, our parts spin as if something is looming. From our parts' perspective, something is happening; however, what they experience is happening in the past where that part is currently stuck, reliving a particular scene again and again. For many who have experienced trauma or complex trauma, it's not an easy task to live without fear. For many people, working with a trained IFS therapist may be necessary to help heal their parts and get relief.

Even though parts hold much of our discomfort, I believe Self can still feel pain, sadness, loss, and grief. When we lose someone or when bad things happen, we can feel the effect and the full range of emotions those events evoke. There's beauty in feeling what is necessary in the moment. Simultaneously, our parts are usually activated, and we feel their pain too. The experience, however, is very different when our parts are activated. Parts grieve with more desperation and loneliness, whereas Self can sit in the grief, rocking with the swells of it. In fact, one of my most beautiful healing experiences happened when I allowed myself to feel grief. I found a part of me who was in the basement of my childhood home. He was outside my brother's bedroom door, sitting on the floor, hugging his knees with his head hung low. My brother died when I was 15 years old after years of fighting cancer. I sat next to that 15-year-old and started to sense that he was grieving alone. No one ever asked him how he was doing during his brother's illness and after his brother died. So I (Self) sat next to him, in the same position. We cried together, rocked together, and held each other. Afterward, we came out of the basement, and he is with me now, integrated into my present life. My brother's death feels much more resolved in my system after that experience.

Being with our parts isn't always that intense, and it's amazing how simple life experiences can be trailheads to get to know our parts. Here's an example of how a simple situation in the present can activate our parts in the past, causing us to feel discomfort. My wife and I were sitting on our deck, and we noticed some mosquitoes. I was sharing how I typically don't mind them, and when I stay calm, they mostly leave me alone. Then I felt a bite on my forehead, and I immediately felt a sinking feeling in my stomach. I went inside the house and felt a bit of panic. I felt an urgency not to have a big bite on my forehead. I sensed a protector was afraid of other people noticing and judging me. Once I saw it in the mirror, I felt that sinking feeling in my stomach again. I took a breath and went inside. I put my attention on that sinking feeling. I then saw myself as a young boy in a cabin our family rented one summer. At that time, I was allergic to mosquito bites, and they would swell up big. I sensed that boy's emotions, and I asked him to show me what he wanted me to know. He was by the fire, and he felt a large bite on his forehead, and I could feel his head begin to ache. He showed me my dad, a vague figure sitting nearby, detached. The scene shifted to him in the kitchen area of the cabin, and my mom was pressing an ice cube on his forehead like she was trying to smash the bite out of existence. Somewhat comforting, but the look in her eye was not with me, not present. She was not emotionally there for me. He was in a family, but he was alone. He started blending with me, and I almost became overwhelmed with his sadness.

I took another deep breath and asked him for just enough space so I could be there with him. I went to the boy in the scene and let him see me. After acknowledging what he was going through, he wanted to be in the present with me. Once he was there, I thought to myself, "Wait! I'm a Dad," and I let that young boy know that. I told him I knew natural remedies for mosquito bites. I did the following steps and talked him through it the whole time. I helped my body how I would help my own kids. I went outside and picked some Plantain leaves (not the bananas, a weed in many people's yards). I crushed them first and then rubbed them on the bite. I grabbed an ice pack and gently held it to my forehead, breathing with him as I did. Finally, I added Eucalyptus oil and reapplied the ice. I talked my young part through it the whole time, letting him know what I was doing, attuning to his needs. He felt at ease with it, and he sensed my confidence and allowed himself to be helped. He felt me there for him, and perhaps for the first time, he felt cared for. I checked in the mirror, and the bite diminished to mostly nothing. I noticed how my nervous system regulated and relaxed. I had no panic, no fear, and I had a lot of spaciousness. I felt him lean into me with his appreciation. That little boy was stuck in time, at that cabin, feeling alone. Now that he had experienced me, I listened to more of his stories. He is here with me now, and he released his burdened beliefs, beliefs like: he wasn't worthy of attention and attunement. Now, he can experience what it is like to get the love and care he always wanted.

This process of being with our parts and retrieving them can happen with all of our parts again and again. It takes time, patience, and oftentimes, hard emotional labor as we feel what these parts need us to feel. Yet, in the end, it's worth it. As our parts heal, it's easier and easier to be Self-led, because the burdens we carry lessen. As Richard Schwartz says, the burdens our parts carry block our access to Self Energy.

So I end this book by inviting you to go inside, be with those sweet parts and give them what they always wanted and needed— someone to see them, believe them, love them, and provide consistency. Listen to them and help them feel understood and appreciated. Bring them to the present when they say they are ready, usually after they've shared everything they've been holding, and help them release the burdened beliefs they carry, take on new roles, and be comforted by you. And most of all, know that love is the healing force within Self Energy. Our parts need love just like we do, and when they allow us, Self, to lead, our parts will obtain the level of loving connection and safety they desire.

And so I wish you: all the best to you and your parts.

References

Argyris, C. (1990). *Overcoming organizational defenses: Facilitating organizational learning.* Boston: Allyn and Bacon.

Csikszentmihalyi, M. (1990). *Flow: The psychology of optimal experience.* Harper & Row.

Detert, J.R., & Burris, E.R. (2007). Leadership behavior and employee voice: Is the door really open? *Academy of Management Journal*, 50(4), 869-884.

Greenleaf, R. K., & Spears, L. C. (2002). *Servant leadership: a journey into the nature of legitimate power and greatness.* Paulist Press.

Herbine-Blank T, Kerpelman D, Sweezy, M. (2015). *Intimacy from the inside out: Courage and compassion in couple therapy* (25th Anniversary Ed). Routledge.

Kahn, W. A. (1990). Psychological conditions of personal engagement and disengagement at work. *Academy of management journal*, 33(4), 692-724.

Kohn, A (2005). *Unconditional parenting: Moving from rewards and punishments to love and reason.* Atria Books.

McConnell, S. (2020). *Somatic internal family systems therapy: Awareness, breath, resonance, movement, and touch in Practice.* North Atlantic Books.

Senge, P. (1990). *The Fifth Discipline: The art and practice of the learning organization.* Random House Books.

Schwartz, R. C. (2001). *Introduction to internal family systems model.* Trailheads Publications.

Schwartz, R. C. (2008). *You are the one you've been waiting for: Bringing courageous love to intimate relationships.* Trailheads Publications.

Schwartz, R.C. & Sweezy, M. (2020). *Internal family systems therapy* (2nd ed.). Guilford Press.

Schwartz, R.C. (2021). *No bad parts: Healing trauma & restoring wholeness with the internal family systems model.* Sounds True.

Sykes, C. (2016). An IFS lens on addiction: Compassion for extreme parts. In M Sweezy & E. L. Ziskind (Eds.), *Innovations and elaborations in internal family systems therapy* (pp.29-48). Routledge.

About the Author

Seth Kopald is a certified Internal Family Systems (IFS) Practitioner. He holds a PhD in Organization Management with a Specialization in Leadership and a Masters in Education. Seth's doctoral research focused on creating safe climates in which people can share their voice and feel heard. Seth is also a trained Montessori teacher for children 2 ½ – 6 years old. He taught preschool children and went on to teach child development and early childhood education at a community college. He spent the next 15 years consulting with not-for-profit child care programs to improve their educational practices. Seth is a devoted parent and has taught parenting and coached parents since 1996.

Seth has been an IFS Practitioner since 2012, and he is an experienced program assistant for IFS level 1, 2, and 3 trainings. He has also been on Richard Schwartz's staff for two different IFS retreats. For his day job, Seth works with individuals and couples to help them gain a more heart-centered life with better communication and authentic relationships. Seth specializes in Self-led Parenting, Spirituality, and Parts Art.

Printed in Great Britain
by Amazon

45847863R00083